SIXTH EDITION

INTERACTIONS

Listening/Speaking

ACCESS

Emily Austin Thrush

Robert Baldwin

Laurie Blass

Interactions Access Listening/Speaking, Sixth Edition

Published by McGraw-Hill ESL/ELT, a business unit of The McGraw-Hill Companies, Inc.,
1221 Avenue of the Americas, New York, NY 10020. Copyright © 2014 by The McGraw-Hill
Companies, Inc. All rights reserved. Printed in the United States of America. Previous editions
© 2007, 2001, and 1995. No part of this publication may be reproduced or distributed in any
form or by any means, or stored in a database or retrieval system, without the prior written
consent of The McGraw-Hill Companies, Inc., including, but not limited to, in any network
or other electronic storage or transmission, or broadcast for distance learning.

Some ancillaries, including electronic and print components, may not be available to customers
outside the United States.

This book is printed on acid-free paper.

2 3 4 5 6 7 8 9 0 DOW/DOW 1 0 9 8 7 6 5 4

ISBN: 978-0-07-339954-6
MHID: 0-07-339954-X

Senior Vice President, Products & Markets: Kurt L. Strand
Vice President, General Manager, Products & Markets: Michael J. Ryan
Vice President, Content Production & Technology Services: Kimberly Meriwether David
Director of Development: Valerie Kelemen
Marketing Manager: Cambridge University Press
Lead Project Manager: Rick Hecker
Senior Buyer: Michael R. McCormick
Designer: Page2, LLC
Cover/Interior Designer: Page2, LLC
Senior Content Licensing Specialist: Keri Johnson
Manager, Digital Production: Janean A. Utley
Compositor: Page2, LLC
Printer: RR Donnelley

Cover photo: Frontpage/Shutterstock.com

All credits appearing on page iv or at the end of the book are considered to be an extension
of the copyright page.

The Internet addresses listed in the text were accurate at the time of publication. The
inclusion of a website does not indicate an endorsement by the authors or McGraw-Hill, and
McGraw-Hill does not guarantee the accuracy of the information presented at these sites.

www.mhhe.com

www.elt.mcgraw-hill.com

A Special Thank You

The Interactions/Mosaic 6th edition team wishes to thank our extended team: teachers, students, administrators, and teacher trainers, all of whom contributed invaluably to the making of this edition.

Maiko Berger, **Ritsumeikan Asia Pacific University**, Oita, Japan • Aaron Martinson, **Sejong Cyber University**, Seoul, Korea • Aisha Osman, Egypt • Amy Stotts, **Chubu University**, Aichi, Japan • Charles Copeland, **Dankook University**, Yongin City, Korea • Christen Savage, **University of Houston**, Texas, USA • Daniel Fitzgerald, **Metropolitan Community College**, Kansas, USA • Deborah Bollinger, **Aoyama Gakuin University**, Tokyo, Japan • Duane Fitzhugh, **Northern Virginia Community College**, Virginia, USA • Gregory Strong, **Aoyama Gakuin University**, Tokyo, Japan • James Blackwell, **Ritsumeikan Asia Pacific University**, Oita, Japan • Janet Harclerode, **Santa Monica College**, California, USA • Jinyoung Hong, **Sogang University**, Seoul, Korea • Lakkana Chaisaklert, **Rajamangala University of Technology Krung Thep**, Bangkok, Thailand • Lee Wonhee, **Sogang University**, Seoul, Korea • Matthew Gross, **Konkuk University**, Seoul, Korea • Matthew Stivener, **Santa Monica College**, California, USA • Pawadee Srisang, **Burapha University**, Chantaburi, Thailand • Steven M. Rashba, **University of Bridgeport**, Connecticut, USA • Sudatip Prapunta, **Prince of Songkla University**, Trang, Thailand • Tony Carnerie, **University of California San Diego**, California, USA

Photo Credits

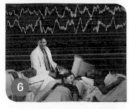

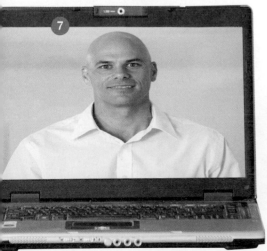

Table of Contents

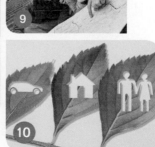

A 21st-Century Course for the Modern Student

Interactions/Mosaic prepares students for university classes by fully integrating every aspect of student life. Based on 28 years of classroom-tested best practices, the new and revised content, fresh modern look, and new online component make this the perfect series for contemporary classrooms.

Proven Instruction that Ensures Academic Success

Modern Content:
From social networking to gender issues and from academic honesty to discussions of Skype, *Interactions/Mosaic* keeps students connected to learning by selecting topics that are interesting and relevant to modern students.

Digital Component
The fully integrated online course offers a rich environment that expands students' learning and supports teachers' teaching with automatically graded practice, assessment, classroom presentation tools, online community, and more.

NEW to *Interactions Access Listening/Speaking* 6th Edition

- **3 Revised Chapters**, updated to reflect contemporary student life:
  Chapter 1: Neighborhoods, Cities, and Towns
  Chapter 3: Friends and Family
  Chapter 5: Men and Women
- **40% new listenings** focus on global topics and digital life
- **Over 60 new vocabulary words** enhance conversational proficiency
- **All new photos** showcase a modern, multi-cultural university experience

Emphasis on Vocabulary:

Each chapter teaches vocabulary intensively and comprehensively. This focus on learning new words is informed by more than 28 years of classroom testing and provides students with the exact language they need to communicate confidently and fluently.

Practical Critical Thinking:

Students develop their ability to synthesize, analyze, and apply information from different sources in a variety of contexts: from comparing academic articles to negotiating informal conversations.

Highlights of *Interactions*
Access Listening/Speaking 6th Edition

Part 1: Conversation Each chapter begins with conversations related to contemporary academic life. The activities that follow help students develop important listening skills.

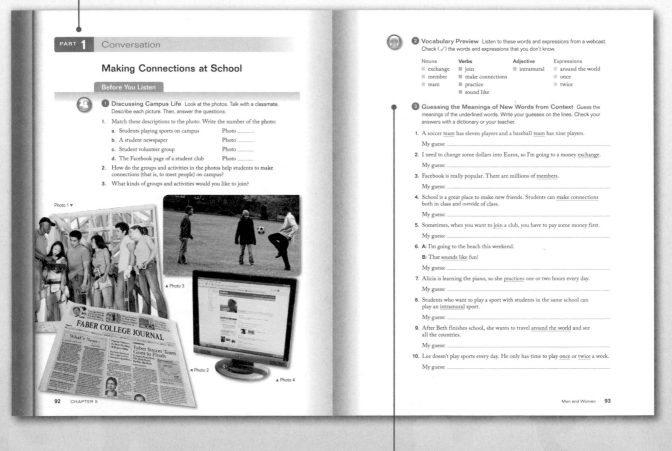

Practical Critical Thinking
Each chapter focuses on a few key strategies for academic and social communication, which support language learning and encourage independence in student thinking.

Part 2: Using Language Students practice taking part in conversations and learn functional language for a variety of conversational settings.

Making Small Talk

FOCUS

What is Small Talk?
"Small talk" is friendly talk you can use to start conversations with people you know and with people you just met. For example, you can talk about the weather.

What are good places and topics for small talk?
Here are good places and topics for small talk and ways you can start:

Place	Topic	Examples
Outside: waiting for the bus	The weather	Nice weather, isn't it? Beautiful day, isn't it? It's really hot today, isn't it? Boy, it's really cold!
Inside: waiting in line	The long line	This line is long, isn't it? This is taking forever, isn't it? I hope we don't have to wait too long!
At a party	The people	Do you know anyone here at the party? Do you know the host? Is this your first time at (host's) place?
At a restaurant, cafeteria, or fast-food place	The place and the food	Nice restaurant, isn't it? The food here is great, isn't it? Is this your first time here? Is the food good? Boy, this place is crowded, isn't it?
At a sports event, a concert, the movies, etc.	Activities related to the event	Are you a (Yankees/Brad Pitt/U2) fan? Do you like this singer? Do you like (action/romance/sci-fi) movies? I think this is going to be a great show! What do you think?

▼ Students waiting for a concert and making small talk

Before You Listen

1 **Small Talk and Short Answer Practice** Follow these steps to practice small talk:

1. Practice the small talk opening examples in the right column on page 100.
2. Ask your classmates and/or your teacher about any words you do not understand.
3. Take turns making small talk with a classmate and giving short "yes" answers to each question.

   Example: **Student 1:** Nice weather, isn't it?

   Student 2: Yes, it is!

Listen

2 **Listening to Small Talk** Listen to four short small talk conversations. Write the number of the conversation under the photo it matches. There is one extra photo. After you listen, use that extra photo to make up a conversation with your partner.

▲ Photo A
Conversation #: _____

▲ Photo B
Conversation #: _____

▲ Photo C
Conversation #: _____

▲ Photo D
Conversation #: _____

▲ Photo E
Conversation #: _____

Communication for the Modern Student
A focus on real-life and academic communication prepares students for success in school and in life.

Part 3: Listening Corresponding audio and impactful exercises help students practice getting meaning from context, a critical skill for navigating conversations.

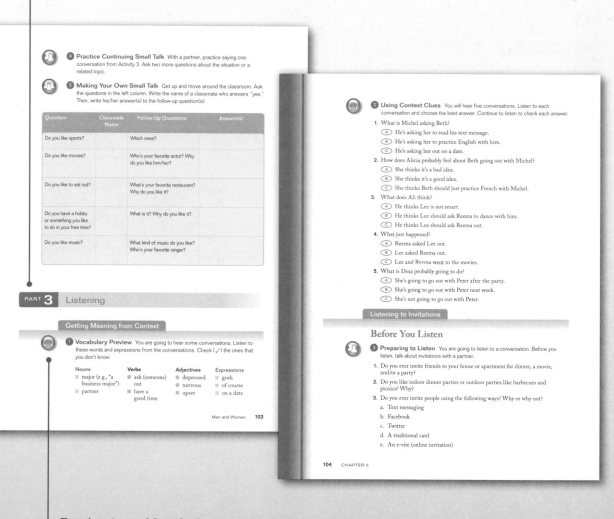

4 Practice Continuing Small Talk With a partner, practice saying one conversation from Activity 3. Ask two more questions about the situation or a related topic.

5 Making Your Own Small Talk Get up and move around the classroom. Ask the questions in the left column. Write the name of a classmate who answers "yes." Then, write his/her answer(s) to the follow-up question(s).

Question	Classmate Name	Follow-Up Questions	Answer(s)
Do you like sports?		Which ones?	
Do you like movies?		Who's your favorite actor? Why do you like him/her?	
Do you like to eat out?		What's your favorite restaurant? Why do you like it?	
Do you have a hobby or something you like to do in your free time?		What is it? Why do you like it?	
Do you like music?		What kind of music do you like? Who's your favorite singer?	

PART 3 Listening

Getting Meaning from Context

1 Vocabulary Preview You are going to hear some conversations. Listen to these words and expressions from the conversations. Check (✓) the ones that you don't know.

Nouns
- major (e.g., "a business major")
- partner

Verbs
- ask (someone) out
- have a good time

Adjectives
- depressed
- nervous
- upset

Expressions
- gosh
- of course
- on a date

Men and Women **103**

2 Using Context Clues You will hear five conversations. Listen to each conversation and choose the best answer. Continue to listen to check each answer.

1. What is Michel asking Beth?
   (A) He's asking her to read his text message.
   (B) He's asking her to practice English with him.
   (C) He's asking her out on a date.
2. How does Alicia probably feel about Beth going out with Michel?
   (A) She thinks it's a bad idea.
   (B) She thinks it's a good idea.
   (C) She thinks Beth should just practice French with Michel.
3. What does Ali think?
   (A) He thinks Lee is not smart.
   (B) He thinks Lee should ask Reema to dance with him.
   (C) He thinks Lee should ask Reema out.
4. What just happened?
   (A) Reema asked Lee out.
   (B) Lee asked Reema out.
   (C) Lee and Reema went to the movies.
5. What is Dina probably going to do?
   (A) She's going to go out with Peter after the party.
   (B) She's going to go out with Peter next week.
   (C) She's not going to go out with Peter.

Listening to Invitations

Before You Listen

3 Preparing to Listen You are going to listen to a conversation. Before you listen, talk about invitations with a partner.

1. Do you ever invite friends to your house or apartment for dinner, a movie, and/or a party?
2. Do you like indoor dinner parties or outdoor parties like barbecues and picnics? Why?
3. Do you ever invite people using the following ways? Why or why not?
   a. Text messaging
   b. Facebook
   c. Twitter
   d. A traditional card
   e. An e-vite (online invitation)

104 CHAPTER 5

Emphasis on Vocabulary Each chapter presents, practices, and carefully recycles vocabulary-learning strategies and vocabulary words essential to the modern student.

Part 4: Speaking Throughout the chapter, graphic organizers and tips help students remember words, language functions and conversational tools. They are now prepared for more extended speaking practice.

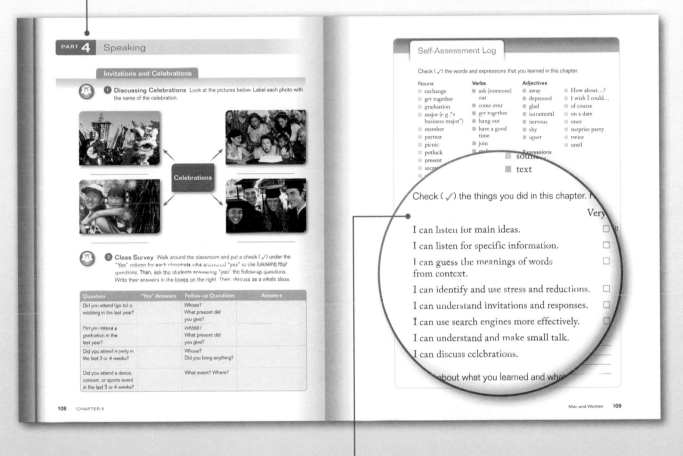

Results for Students A carefully structured program presents and practices academic skills and strategies purposefully, leading to strong student results and more independent learners.

Scope and Sequence

Critical-Thinking Skills	Vocabulary Building	Pronunciation	Language Skills
Using a T-chart to compare two things Comparing and contrasting Using Internet search engines and keywords to find and evaluate information Interpreting a photo	Terms for college life and campuses Terms for contact information Getting meaning from context Terms about neighborhood and city life Expressions for giving directions	Listening for and using stress in words and sentences	Using contractions Using expressions for giving directions to places
Developing reasoning skills for argumentation Interpreting information on shopping websites Using charts to compare and contrast	Shopping terms Price expressions Clothing types and colors Guessing meaning from context	Using reductions Listening for and using stressed words	Describing clothing Using monetary terms for prices
Researching words online Identifying relationships based on greeting	Terms for staying in touch using technology Terms for types of greetings Expressions for leaving voicemails Expressions for describing people	Listening for and using stressed words and reduced forms of words	Starting and ending conversations Leaving voicemail messages
Analyzing solutions to problems Making comparisons Interpreting photos Using charts to organize information	Words and expressions for discussing health care Words and expressions for making healthcare appointments Guessing meaning from context Body part terms	Listening for and using stressed words Listening for reductions Using online pronunciation dictionaries	Using modals to give advice

Scope and Sequence

Critical-Thinking Skills	Vocabulary Building	Pronunciation	Language Skills
Interpreting photos Using keywords and search engines to find information effectively	Terms for campus life and activities Expressions for describing personal feelings Terms for dating and social events	Listening for and using stressed words and reductions with *did you*	Patterns for small talk Giving, accepting, and refusing invitations
Understanding and interpreting research studies Evaluating important lecture points with note-taking Understanding and using data to support a point	Expressions for agreeing and disagreeing Understanding basic vocabulary used in research studies Transition vocabulary for narratives Guessing meaning from context	Stress: teens and tens Listening for and using stressed words	Polite and impolite ways to agree and disagree
Interpreting photos Categorizing people and things Interpreting survey results Using a cluster chart graphic organizer to group related ideas Evaluating career information on the Internet Using a chart or pie graph to illustrate survey results	Words and expressions for discussing jobs and careers Job titles and major terms Job interview terms Guessing meaning from context	Listening for and using stressed words Distinguishing majors and job titles	Making complaints
Making comparison charts Ordering steps in a sequence Evaluating search information on the Internet	Words and expressions for discussing food and nutrition Guessing meaning from context Words and expressions for giving a sequence	Listening for and using stressed words	Using sequencing words Using present tense to talk about food preferences

Scope and Sequence

Critical-Thinking Skills	Vocabulary Building	Pronunciation	Language Skills
Evaluating options and making decisions with a T-chart Classifying information	Describing places and events Travel terms Guessing meaning from context	Listening for and using stressed words	Using modals and expressions to persuade Using past tense to talk about travel
Interpreting photos Categorizing pros and cons with a T-chart Interpreting persuasive messages Finding information about the environment on the Internet	Words and expressions for discussing the environment and endangered species Terms of persuasion Guessing meaning from context	Listening for and using stressed words Using stressed words for emphasis	Using present tense to agree and disagree Using the imperative to give advice

Introducing the Interactions Access Listening/Speaking Characters

Name: Ali
Nationality: American

Name: Beth
Nationality: American

Name: Ming
Nationality: Chinese

Name: Dan
Nationality: American

Name: Lee
Nationality: Korean

Name: Alicia
Nationality: Mexican

Name: Peter
Nationality: Puerto Rican

Name: Alex
Nationality: Mexican

1 Neighborhoods, Cities, and Towns

> "No city should
> be too large for
> a man to walk
> out of in
> a morning."
>
> Cyril Connolly
> English writer

In this
CHAPTER

Using Language
- Asking for and Giving Personal Information
- Confirming Information

Listening
- Listening to Descriptions of Neighborhoods
- Listening to Directions

Speaking
- Talking About Places on Campus

Connecting to the Topic

1. Look at the photo. Describe the people and the place that you see.

2. Beth, Ali, and Lee are students at Faber College. Do you think Faber College is in a big city or a small town? Why?

3. Where do you go to school? Is it in a big city or a small town?

Where Are You From?

Strategy

Using a T-Chart
A T-chart is a chart with two sides. T-charts help you compare two things. You can easily see similarities and differences when two pieces of information are next to each other.

Before You Listen

1 Comparing Two Colleges Look at the photos. Talk with a classmate. Compare the two schools. Use the T-chart on page 5 to help you with your discussion. Use the words in the box and your own ideas.

Nouns

air	city	lifestyle	town	transportation
buildings	concrete	people	traffic	trees

Adjectives

big	clean	exciting	polluted	rural	tall
busy	crowded	noisy	quiet	small	urban

▲ An urban campus   ▲ A rural campus

A Rural Campus	A Urban Campus
a lot of trees	*a lot of buildings*

Expressions
There are some/a lot of/many… There aren't any/many/a lot of…

Examples:

There are a lot of trees on a rural campus. There aren't many tall buildlings.

There are a lot of city buildings and streets on an urban campus. There aren't many trees.

2 Vocabulary Preview   Listen to these words and expressions from a webcast. Check (✓) the words and expressions that you don't know.

Nouns	Verb	Adjectives		Expression
▦ activities	▦ miss	▦ comfortable	▦ normal	▦ How do you
▦ campus		▦ excited	▦ pretty	feel about…?
		▦ nervous	▦ quiet	

3 Guessing the Meanings of New Words from Context   Guess the meanings of the underlined words and expressions. Write your guesses on the lines. Check your answers with a dictionary or with your teacher.

1. I don't see my friends very much, and that makes me sad. I really <u>miss</u> them!

   My guess: _____

2. There are a lot of <u>activities</u> at my school. There are sports, clubs, and parties.

   My guess: _____

3. **A:** <u>How do you feel about</u> your new school? **B:** Happy! I really like it here!

   My guess: _____

4. My town is very <u>quiet</u>. It's not noisy like a big city.

   My guess: _____

5. Princeton University is very <u>pretty</u> because it has a lot of trees and flowers. Trees and flowers always make a school look nice.

   My guess: _____

6. **A:** I don't like noisy places. **B:** That's <u>normal</u>. A lot of people don't like noisy places.

   My guess: _____

7. New students at Faber College sometimes feel very <u>nervous</u>. They're worried because life is so different here.

My guess: _____

8. I'm <u>comfortable</u> in big cities because I live in New York. I feel happy where there are a lot of people, buildings, and noise.

My guess: _____

9. She's <u>excited</u> about studying at Faber College because it's a good school.

My guess: _____

10. Because I live on the Faber College <u>campus</u>, I'm near my classes and I meet a lot of other students.

My guess: _____

Listen

 4 **Listening for Main Ideas** Listen to the first part of the webcast and choose the best answer to each question.

1. Why is Alex talking to Beth, Ali, and Lee?
   - Ⓐ They miss their friends.
   - Ⓑ They like campus activities.
   - Ⓒ They're new students.

2. What are they talking about?
   - Ⓐ what they are studying
   - Ⓑ why they are studying at Faber College
   - Ⓒ where they are from

3. Why is Ali nervous?
   - Ⓐ His classes are difficult.
   - Ⓑ He doesn't go away from home a lot.
   - Ⓒ He's a new student.

 5 **Listening for Specific Information** Listen to the complete webcast and choose the correct answer to each question.

1. Why does Lee like Faber College?
   - Ⓐ There's a lot of nightlife.
   - Ⓑ It's like Seoul.
   - Ⓒ It's quiet and there are a lot of trees.

2. What does Alex tell Ali?
   - Ⓐ He (Alex) is nervous too.
   - Ⓑ Most students don't feel nervous.
   - Ⓒ It's normal to be nervous.

3. What place is Beth's hometown like?
   - (A) Seoul
   - (B) Silver Spring
   - (C) the town that Faber College is in

4. What do a lot of new students miss?
   - (A) campus activities
   - (B) friends from home
   - (C) sports and clubs

5. Why does Beth say, "I miss my friends, too, Ali"?
   - (A) to make him feel comfortable
   - (B) to make him feel nervous
   - (C) to make him feel sorry

After You Listen

6 **Vocabulary Review** Complete the conversation. Use words from the box.

activities	campus	comfortable	excited	feel
miss	nervous	normal	pretty	quiet

Dan: So Peter, how do you _____ about Faber College?

1

Peter: I really like the _____. It looks very nice. How do *you* feel?

2

Dan: I like Faber, too. You're right. It's _____ because of all

3

the trees. And it's like my hometown, so I feel very _____

4

here.

Peter: It's a very _____ town—not like my hometown. There

5

isn't much to do at night here at Faber.

Dan: Yes, but there's a lot to do here during the day. There are a lot of

_____ here, like sports.

6

Peter: You're right. Do you _____ your old friends? You don't see

7

them now, right?

Dan: No. Actually, two of my friends are here. I'm lucky!

Peter: Yes, you are. So, how do you feel about your classes?

Dan: I'm _____ about my classes. They're really interesting.

8

How about you?

Peter: I'm a little _____. I'm worried because I'm taking
9

Introduction to Accounting. It's hard for me.

Dan: That's _____. I worry about some of my classes too.
10

But you're smart, Peter, so don't worry so much!

Stress

Stressing Words in English

In English conversation, some words are *stressed*. We say stressed words louder and more clearly than other words. We stress words for different reasons. Understanding stressed words helps you to understand and speak English better.

Example

Where   are   you   from?

(stressed)   (stressed)

In this book, you will practice listening for stress.

7 **Listening for Stressed Words** Listen to the first part of the webcast again. The stressed words are marked.

Alex: Hello everyone. Welcome to Faber College Webcast. My name is Alex. Today, I'm talking to three new students at Faber. So, where are you from?

Ali: I'm from Silver Spring, Maryland.

Alex: Wow! That's near a big city—Washington D.C.

Lee: And I'm from Seoul, Korea.

Alex: That's a big city, too. Faber is in a small town. How do you feel about living here?

Lee: I'm excited. I like the campus. It's pretty and quiet. There are so many trees!

Alex: What about you, Ali?

Ali: Not really. In fact, I'm a little nervous. This is my first time away from home.

8 **Marking Stressed Words** Now listen to more of the webcast. This time, mark the stressed words that you hear.

Alex: That's very normal. A lot of students feel nervous at first. Now, Beth, you're from a small town, right?

Beth: Yes. I come from San Anselmo. It's a small town in Northern California.

Alex: What's it like?

Beth: Well, it's a lot like this town, so I'm very comfortable here.

Alex: Great! Now, a lot of new students miss their friends from home. What about you?

Ali: Yeah, I really miss my friends.

Beth: I miss my friends, too, Ali, but there's a lot to do at Faber College—sports, clubs…

Contractions

Combining Words with Contractions

Contractions are a way to combine words. People use contractions in writing and in speaking. When you write contractions, you drop letters and replace those letters with an apostrophe ('). When you say contractions, you drop sounds.

Long Form	Contraction
I am from Seoul	**I'm** from Seoul.
That is near a big city.	**That's** near a big city.
It is pretty and quiet.	**It's** pretty and quiet.

9 **Comparing Long Forms and Contractions** Listen to the following sentences from the webcast. Repeat the sentences after the speaker.

Long Form	Contraction
I am from Silver Spring.	I'm from Silver Spring.
That is near a big city.	That's near a big city.
There are so many trees!	There're* so many trees!
It is pretty and quiet.	It's pretty and quiet.
What is it like?	What's it like?
There is a lot to do at Faber College.	There's a lot to do at Faber College.

* This contraction is not used in writing.

10 **Listening for Contractions** Listen to the sentences. Circle the letter of the sentence you hear.

1. a. There are a lot of activities on campus. b. There're* a lot of activities on campus.
2. a. She is from a small town. b. She's from a small town.
3. a. What is your name? b. What's your name?
4. a. It is noisy here! b. It's noisy here!

5. a. I am from Silver Spring. b. I'm from Silver Spring.
6. a. San Anselmo is a small town. b. San Anselmo's a small town.
7. a. There is a lot of noise in here. b. There's a lot of noise in here.
8. a. He is from New York City. b. He's from New York City.

Using the Internet

Finding Information Online

You can use the Internet to practice listening and speaking. To find listening and speaking websites, use *keywords*. Keywords are words that are related to your topic. For example, if you want to find websites that help with English pronunciation, type the keywords "English pronunciation" to get a list of sites.

Example

| English pronunciation | Submit |

After you do a search, the next step is choosing useful sites. One way to choose a useful site is to read the site description. Look for words in the description that tell you if a site is useful. For example, if you want intermediate level pronunciation activities, look for the word *intermediate* in the site description.

Which sites below are good for **students**? Which site is good for **teachers**? Which one is probably **free**? Which one is for **advanced** students? If you are a beginning student and don't want to pay, the circled site is probably the most useful for you.

- Listening Skills Lessons | LessonPlanet.com
  www.lessonplanet.com
  Find listening skills lessons from 200,000 teacher lesson plans
- Randall's ESL Cyber Listening Lab–For English as a Second Language Students
  www.esl-lab.com/
  This free ESL listening website created by Randall Davis helps ESL/EFL students of ALL levels improve their listening comprehension skills through practice with self-grading…
- Advanced English Listening Activities for IELTS students
  www.esolcourses.com/ielts/listening/ielts-video-listening-quiz-2.html
  Advanced level English video quiz, for upper intermediate and IELTS students. Watch a video clip and then answer a variety of different questions about…
- Free English listening activities, English listening skills exercises…
  www.123listening.com/freeaudio.php
  Free English listening worksheets, listening activities and English listening worksheets to print!

11 Practicing Your Search Skills List possible keywords for the following situations:

Situation 1: You want to practice English pronunciation: _____

_____

Situation 2: You want to practice English contractions: _____

_____

Situation 3: You want to practice English stress: _____

_____

Situation 4: Your idea: _____

_____

Now choose situation 1, 2, 3, or 4 above. Use the keywords you wrote and do an online search. Then write the names of the first four results.

1. _____

2. _____

3. _____

4. _____

Answer these questions.

1. Which site is most useful to you? Why? Circle it.

2. Is there a site that is not useful at all? Why? Put an X through it.

Talk It Over

12 Getting to Know You Follow the steps to get to know your classmates.

1. Look at the questions in the chart on page 12. Add your own questions, if you want.

2. Practice asking your questions. Think about stress and contractions.

3. Walk around the room. Ask at least three people the questions. Write their answers in the chart.

4. Share your answers with the class.

Question	Name	Name	Name	Name
	Lisa _____	_____	_____	_____
Where are you from?	Oakville			
Is it a big city or a small town?	It's a small town.			
How many people live there?	About 3,000 people live there.			
How do you feel about living here?	I like it.			
Why? (Explain your answer to question 4.)	It's quiet.			
Do you miss your friends?	No.			
Your question:				

Asking for and Giving Contact Information

FOCUS

Your Personal Information

Sometimes you must give your contact (personal) information. Contact information includes your name, your address, your phone number, and your email address. Sometimes you give your contact information when:

- you meet a new friend
- you are signing up for a class or an activity
- you go to a doctor or a dentist for the first time
- you apply for a job
- someone is sending you something

Example:

A: What is your name and address?

B: Jason Ganrick, 542 Ellsworth Street,
Apartment 2R,
San Francisco, California

A: What's your zip code?

B: 94933.

A: What's your phone number?

B: 415-555-9685.

A: Got it!

▲ Applying for a job: What is your name and address?

Note: Sometimes you *don't* want to give your contact information. Situations include:

- at a party
- to a stranger

Here are some things to say when you don't want to give your contact information:

A: What's your email address?

B: I'd rather not say.
OR
I'm afraid I don't give out my email address or phone number.
OR
Sorry. I don't give out personal information.

▲ At a restaurant: What's your email address? Or your phone number?

1 **Listening for Contact Information** Listen to the conversations. Write the information that you hear. If the person doesn't give the information, write X.

1. First name: _____Michael_____ Last name: _____Green_____

   Address: _____ _____Grand Avenue,_____ _____Apartment_____ _____

   Phone number: (_____)_____

2. First name: _____ Last name: _____

   Address: __P.O. Box__ _____ ____Brooklyn, NY____ _____

   Email address: _____@_____.com

3. First name: _____ Last name: _____

   Address: _____ ____Oak Street,____ ____Los Angeles, CA____ _____

   Phone number: (_____)_____

   Email address: _____

4. First name: _____ Last name: _____

   Phone number: (_____)_____

2 **Writing Contact Information** Write information about yourself.

● ● ●	
◄ ► + ● www.mymail.com/contacts	🔍▾ ⟳
🔍 Search GO	HOME PAGE MY ACCOUNT HELP CALENDAR MORE

MyMail   ←   ✉   ⊘

CONTACTS

Address Book
New Group

First Name [   ]

Last Name [   ]

Address [   ]

Phone Number [   ]

Email Address [   ]

(Add)

3 **Asking for and Giving Contact Information** Work with a partner. Ask your partner the contact information questions. Then switch roles.

Example:

Student A: What's your name?

Student B: My name is Oscar Sandoval.

Student A: What's your address?

Student B: My address is 1345 University Avenue, San Diego, California, 92103

Student A: What's your phone number?

Student B: It's (515) 555-7869.

Student A: What's your email address?

Student B: It's osandoval@ials.com

Strategy

Confirming Information

Sometimes you are not sure that you are hearing contact information correctly. If you are not sure, you can repeat the information as a question.

Example: **Ms. Dunn:** What is your telephone number?
Michael Green: My number is (415) 555-7950.
Ms. Dunn: (415) 555-7950?
Michael Green: That's right.

4 **Asking for and Confirming Contact Information** Walk around the room. Ask your classmates the questions you practiced in Activity **3**. Write down the names, addresses, phone numbers, and email addresses of four classmates. To make sure you hear information correctly, confirm it with your classmate. If you don't want to give out your personal information, use the expressions in the box on page 13.

Example:

Student A: What's your address?

Student B: 4562 Mission Road, San Marcos, California, 92069.

Student A: 92069?

Student B: That's right.

	Name	Name	Name	Name
	_____	_____	_____	_____
Contact Information				

Getting Meaning from Context

Before You Listen

1 **Prelistening Questions** Discuss these questions with your class. Talk about your school or a school you know.

1. Is the school big or small? How many students are there?

2. If students need money, do they go to an ATM (an automated teller machine) or to the bank? Are there ATMs near the school?

3. Talk about some of the places on the campus or near the school: Is there a library? Where is it? Is there a Student Union? What do people do there? Is there a café?

4. How do most students get to school? Do they take the bus? The subway? Do they walk?

5. Look at the photo of Florida State University (FSU) in Tallahassee, Florida. Describe what you see on the picture. Talk about the following:

   - the students
   - plants (trees and flowers)
   - the buildings
   - the weather

After you describe the photo, discuss your answers to these questions with the class.

1. What is the student lifestyle probably like at FSU? Give reasons for your answer.

2. Do you want to go to a school like FSU? Why or why not?

▲ Florida State University campus

Listen

2 **Using Context Clues** You will hear five conversations. Listen to each conversation and choose the best answer.

1. What is the University of California like?
   - (A) It's like Faber College.
   - (B) It's a big school.
   - (C) It's a small school.
   - (D) It has 14,000 students.

2. What does Ali think about his Art History class?
   - (A) It's hard.
   - (B) It's easy.
   - (C) It's boring.
   - (D) It's interesting.

3. Where is Beth going?
   - (A) to the bank
   - (B) to the Student Union
   - (C) to the café
   - (D) to the gym

4. Where is the English Department?
   - (A) next to the library
   - (B) next to the café
   - (C) across from the Student Union
   - (D) the next building

5. Why doesn't Beth take the bus?
   - (A) She thinks the bus is too crowded.
   - (B) She thinks the bus stop is too far.
   - (C) She thinks the bus takes too long.
   - (D) She wants to get some exercise.

Before You Listen

3 **Prelistening Questions** You are going to listen to a conversation. Before you listen, look at the pictures and discuss the questions below with a partner.

◄ Neighborhood A

◄ Neighborhood B

1. Describe the two neighborhoods. What is life like in each neighborhood?

2. What are the good things (the pros) and the bad things (the cons) about living in each neighborhood? Complete the pro/con T-chart.

	Pros	Cons
Neighborhood A		
Neighborhood B		*noisy*

3. Which kind of neighborhood do you prefer? Why? Give three reasons.

4 Vocabulary Preview Listen to these words and phrases. Check (✓) the ones that you don't know.

Nouns
- neighbors
- public
- transportation
- traffic

Adjectives
- boring
- convenient
- ethnic (shops, restaurants)

Expressions
- at the end of my block
- on my block

Listen

5 Listening for the Main Idea Listen to the conversation and circle the best word to complete the statement.

The woman thinks her neighborhood is **better/worse** than the man's neighborhood.

6 Listening for Details Listen again. What does the woman like about South Beach? What doesn't she like about her neighborhood? What does the man like about Little Gables? What doesn't he like about his neighborhood? Complete the pro/con T-chart for the two neighborhoods in the conversation.

	Pros	Cons
South Beach	*ethnic restaurants*	
Little Gables		

After You Listen

7 Discussing Neighborhoods Talk about the answers to these questions in small groups.

1. What is your neighborhood like? Describe it to your classmates. Use the words from this chapter and your own ideas.

2. Describe a good neighborhood for each type of person:
   - an elderly couple
   - two college students
   - a young family
   - two successful young professionals

Before You Listen

Strategy

Visualizing

When you listen to directions, it's a good idea to **visualize** them. That is, "see" a picture in your mind of the directions and the places the speaker talks about. For example, if the speaker says, "Go straight on this street and then turn right. The café is next to the theater" make a map in your mind as you listen.

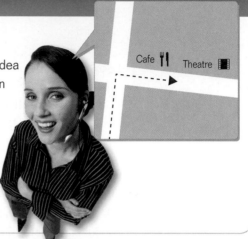

8 Vocabulary Preview Listen to these expressions for giving directions. Listen to the directions. Visualize and draw them in the space provided as you listen.

turn right	go straight	on your left	next to
turn left	stay on...	on your right	

9 **Listening for the Main Idea** Listen to the conversation and circle the correct answer to the question.

Does the man understand the woman's directions?

Yes   No

Listen

10 **Listening for Specific Information** Listen again. Draw a line to follow the woman's directions. Compare your map with a partner's.

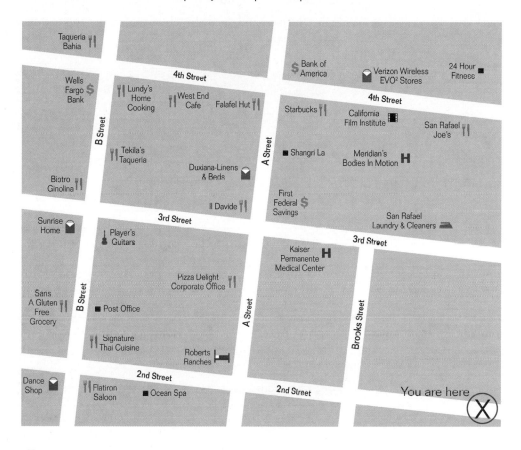

11 **Checking Directions** Listen again and check your answer to Activity 10.

12 **Listening to and Giving Directions** Now use the map above and take turns giving your partner directions to the following places on the map. Start at the California Film Institute. Use your finger to follow the directions that you hear.

- Kaiser Permanente Medical Center
- Wells Fargo Bank
- Signature Thai Cuisine
- San Rafael Laundry & Cleaners
- Dance Shop

After You Listen

13 Getting Directions Answer the questions.

1. How do you usually get directions? Check (✓) the ones you use.

   _____ ask people

   _____ use a street map

   _____ print directions from the Internet

   _____ use GPS (global positioning system) in a car

   _____ use GPS on a phone

2. What are the pros and cons of each of these ways to get directions? Complete the pro/con chart.

	Pros	Cons
Asking people		sometimes people don't understand me
Using a street map		
Printing directions from the Internet		
Using GPS in a car		
Using GPS on a phone		

3. Get into small groups and compare your pro/con charts. Then discuss your answer to this question: Which ways of getting directions are best for which situations? Talk about three situations with your group. Use your own ideas or ideas from the box.

visiting a new city   planning a trip   lost in your own city   giving directions

Example:

A: Asking people for directions is best when you're visiting a new city.

B: But it's dangerous to talk to strangers!

C: I don't think so. And it's a good way to practice your English.

Talking About Places on Campus

1 **Talking About Maps** Look at the map and answer these questions.
Then compare your answers with a partner.

1. What kind of map is this? How do you know?

2. Name five buildings you see. What activities happen in each building you and your partner named?

3. Where can you find a map like this?

4 What are some reasons that people need a map like this?

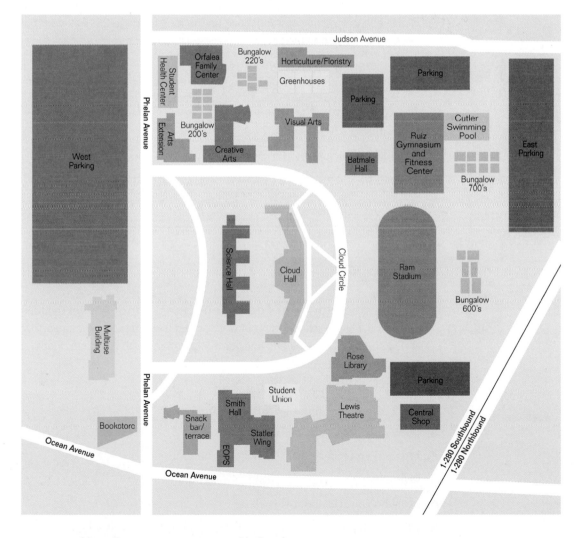

Now discuss your answers with the class.

2 **Understanding a Campus Map** Work with a partner. Find these places on the campus map on page 23:

on page 23

a. Where do you go to buy books? _____ *the bookstore* _____

b. Where do you go to borrow books? _____

c. Where do you go to get a snack? _____

d. Where are the science classes? _____

e. Where do you go if you get sick? _____

f. Where can you exercise? _____

g. Where do you park your car? _____

h. Where do you go to see a student performance? _____

3 **Role-Play** Find any starting place on the map on page 23. Ask your partner directions to three of the following places. Then switch roles.

the library	east parking lot	the swimming pool
the science building	the bookstore	the student union

Example:

Student A: Excuse me. How do I get to the bookstore?

Student B: Go straight on Judson Avenue. Turn left on Phelan Ave. The bookstore is close to Ocean Avenue, across from the snack bar and terrace.

Student A: Thanks!

Putting It Together

4 **Discussing How You Feel About Something** Answer the following questions. Give a reason for your answer and try to use the vocabulary you learned in this chapter. Then ask and answer the questions with a partner. Finally, share your answers with the class.

1. How do you feel about this class?

2. How do you feel about learning English?

3. How do you feel about your school?

4. How do you feel about your neighborhood?

Example:

A: How do you feel about this class?

B: I feel excited because I'm going to learn a lot. How do *you* feel?

B: I feel nervous about learning English because it's hard.

A: I think that's normal.

Self-Assessment Log

Check (✓) the words and expressions that you learned in this chapter.

Nouns
- activities
- campus
- neighbors
- public
- transportation
- traffic

Verb
- miss

Adjectives
- boring
- comfortable
- convenient
- ethnic (shops, restaurants)
- excited
- nervous

- normal
- pretty
- quiet

Expressions
- at the end of my block
- How do you feel about…?
- on my block

Check (✓) the things you did in this chapter. How well can you do each one?

	Very well	Fairly well	Not very well
I can listen for main ideas.	☐	☐	☐
I can listen for specific information.	☐	☐	☐
I can guess the meanings of words from context.	☐	☐	☐
I can listen for and use stress and contractions.	☐	☐	☐
I can choose useful sites on the Internet.	☐	☐	☐
I can ask for and give personal information.	☐	☐	☐
I can confirm information.	☐	☐	☐
I can use a T-chart to compare things.	☐	☐	☐
I can talk about places on campus.	☐	☐	☐
I can describe neighborhoods.	☐	☐	☐
I can listen to and give directions.	☐	☐	☐

Write about what you learned and what you did in this chapter.

In this chapter,

I learned _____

_____

I liked _____

_____

CHAPTER 2

Shopping and E-Commerce

"If you can't smile,
don't open a store."

Chinese proverb

In this
CHAPTER

Using Language
Giving Reasons

Listening
Listening for Prices • Listening to Online Shopping Information

Speaking
Talking About Clothes • Comparing Prices

Connecting to the Topic

1. Where are Alicia, Beth, and Ali? What do you think they are doing?

2. Where do you like to shop? What do you like to shop for?

3. Do you shop online? What do you buy online?

Shopping

1 **Comparing Online Shopping to Traditional Shopping** Look at these photos. How are the two ways of shopping different? How are they similar? Talk to a classmate. Use the chart below to help with your discussion. Put your answers in the appropriate column.

Features	Shopping in a Store	Shopping Online
Where: Indoors? Outdoors?		
When: Anytime? Only during store hours?		
What do you need to shop?: A car or other transportation? A computer? Internet access?		
How do you shop?: Talk to a salesperson? Give personal information? Try (on) a product before buying? Window-shop (browse) without buying anything?		
How can you pay?: By cash? By credit card? By ATM (bank) card? By traveler's check?		

▼ Shopping in a store

Shopping online ▶

2 Prelistening Questions Look at the photo. Ali and Beth are at Alicia's apartment. Alicia is also a student at Faber College. Answer the questions with a classmate.

1. Alicia just opened her apartment door. What do you think Alicia says to Ali and Beth?
2. What do you think Beth says to Alicia?
3. Alicia doesn't know Ali. What is Beth saying to introduce Alicia and Ali?
4. Why do you think Beth and Ali are at Alicia's apartment?

3 Vocabulary Preview Listen to these words and expressions from Ali, Beth, and Alicia's conversation. Check (✓) the words and expressions that you don't know.

Noun	Verbs	Adjective	Expression
▦ mall	▦ browse	▦ crowded	▦ No problem!
	▦ look around		
	▦ look for (parking)		
	▦ save money/time/ energy/gas		
	▦ spend money/time		
	▦ try (on)		

4 Guessing the Meanings of New Words from Context Guess the meanings of the underlined words. Write your guesses on the lines. Check your answers with a dictionary or your teacher.

1. Too many people shop at this place—this store is too underlined crowded!

   My guess: _____

2. Alicia can save gas if she doesn't drive her car.

   My guess: _____

3. I like to shop at the mall because there are a lot of different stores there.

   My guess: _____

4. The parking garage is full, so Ali is going to look for parking on the street.

   My guess: _____

5. I can't go shopping because I can't spend any money.

   My guess: _____

6. Beth and Ali don't have any money, so they're just going to look around in some stores and not buy anything.

   My guess: _____

7. Alicia is going to try on the dress to see if it's the right size.

   My guess: _____

8. Alicia likes to browse—sometimes it's fun to look but not buy anything.

   My guess: _____

9. **A:** Can I try on this dress?

   B: Sure, no problem!

   My guess: _____

Listen

5 Listening for Main Ideas (Part 1) Listen to the first part of the conversation. Choose the best answer to each question.

1. Where are Beth and Ali?

   (A) They're at Beth's apartment.

   (B) They're at a store.

   (C) They're at Alicia's apartment.

2. Beth introduces Ali to Alicia. Then, what do Beth, Ali, and Alicia do?

   (A) They enter Alicia's apartment.

   (B) They have some coffee and soda.

   (C) They go shopping.

3. What kind of shopping does Alicia usually do?

    Ⓐ She doesn't know.

    Ⓑ She goes window-shopping with Beth.

    Ⓒ She shops online.

6 Listening for Main Ideas (Part 2) Now listen to the whole conversation. Choose the best answer to each question.

1. Why does Alicia like online shopping?

    Ⓐ The clothes are cheaper.

    Ⓑ It saves time.

    Ⓒ She can try on clothes.

2. What do Beth and Ali dislike (not like) about online shopping?

    Ⓐ They have to drive and look for parking.

    Ⓑ It's so crowded these days.

    Ⓒ They can't touch and try on things they want to buy.

3. What are Beth, Ali, and Alicia going to do?

    Ⓐ They're going to stay at Alicia's apartment and shop online.

    Ⓑ They're going to go shopping at a mall and spend some money.

    Ⓒ They're going to go window-shopping and not spend any money.

7 Listening for Specific Information Listen again. Choose the best answer to each question.

1. Beth introduces Alicia to Ali. Alicia says, "It's nice to meet you." What does Ali say?

    Ⓐ "How are you?"

    Ⓑ "Nice to meet you, too."

    Ⓒ "Nice meeting you."

2. What does Alicia offer Beth and Ali?

    Ⓐ coffee or soda

    Ⓑ water or tea

    Ⓒ water and a seat

3. Ali asks Alicia, "Why do you want to sit in front of a computer screen?" Why does he ask this?

    Ⓐ because it's a nice day

    Ⓑ because Ali wants Alicia to go window-shopping

    Ⓒ both a and b

Strategy

Graphic Organizer: Compare and Contrast Chart

A compare and contrast chart is a good way to look at the positive (pro) and negative (con) points of two or more subjects. Look at the example below comparing bicycles and cars.

	Pro	Con
Bicycles	clean good exercise cheap	slow
Cars	fast	make air dirty expensive

8 **Using a Compare and Contrast Chart to Understand Main Ideas** What do Beth, Ali, and Alicia say about shopping in a store and shopping online? Fill in the chart below with a partner. Add your ideas. Then share your ideas with the class.

	Pro	Con
Shopping in a Store		
Shopping Online	*saves time*	

9 **Vocabulary Review** Complete the sentences on page 33. Use words from the box. Some words may be used more than once. Some sentences have two possible answers.

browse	look around	mall	online shopping	spend
crowded	look for	no problem	save	try on

1. Do you want to buy something at the mall or do you just want to _____?

2. I'm going to the mall just to _____; I'm not going to buy anything.

3. _____ is easy, but you need a computer.

4. We want to shop for three different things, so let's go to the _____.

5. Ali needs to _____ parking before he can go into the mall.

6. I don't have a lot of money, so I don't want to _____ it.

7. Alicia likes to _____ time. She does a lot of online shopping because it's fast.

8. Beth wants to _____ these pants before she buys them.

9. This store is so _____! I don't like it when there are so many people.

10. **A:** I'd like to try on these pants.

    B: Okay, _____!

Stress

10 **Listening for Stressed Words** Listen to a part of the conversation again. The words in the box below are stressed. Fill in the blanks with the words from the box. Some words may be used more than once.

Ali	good	meet	seat
doing	How	nice	Thanks
in	please	too	

Alicia: Hi, Beth. Come on _____.
                                                                1

Beth: Hi, Alicia! _____ are you _____?
                                    2   3

Alicia: Pretty _____.
                              4

Beth: Alicia, this is my friend _____. He's from Silver
                                                          5
Spring, Maryland.

Alicia: Hi, Ali. It's _____ to _____ you.
                                    6   7

Ali: Nice to meet you, _____.
                                          8

Alicia: Well, _____ come _____ and have
                            9   10
a _____.
        11

Beth, Ali: _____!
                          12

Now read the conversation with a group of three. Practice stressing words.

Reductions

Strategy

Understanding Reductions

When speaking, English speakers do not say all words clearly—they use a reduced form or **reduction**. We do not usually use reductions in writing.

Long Form	Reduced Form
I **don't know.**	I **dunno*.**
Do you **want to** look online?	Do you **wanna*** look online?
Where are you going?	**Where're*** you going?

11 **Comparing Long and Reduced Forms** Listen to the following sentences from the conversation. They contain reduced forms. Repeat the sentences after the speaker. Note that the reduced forms (*) are not correct written forms of words.

Long Form	**Reduced Form**
1. How are you doing?	1. How're* you doing?
2. It's nice to meet you.	2. It's nice to meetchya*.
3. We are going to go shopping.	3. We're gonna* go shopping.
4. Do you want to come?	4. Do ya* wanna* come?
5. You don't have to look for parking.	5. You don't hafta* look for parking.

12 **Listening for Reductions** Listen and circle the letter of the sentence that you hear. Note that the reduced forms (*) are not correct written forms of words.

1. **a.** It's nice to meet you.   **b.** It's nice to meetchya.*
2. **a.** Aren't you coming?   **b.** Arencha* comin'?
3. **a.** I'm spending too much money.   **b.** I'm spendin'* too much money.
4. **a.** Do you want to go shopping?   **b.** Do you wanna* go shopping?
5. **a.** Do you have to study today?   **b.** Do you hafta* study today?

*Note that the reduced forms are not correct written forms of words.

Using the Internet

Evaluating Search Results

When you do a search on the Internet, you often get a long list of websites. You don't have time to look at every one. How can you decide if a site is useful? You can tell a lot about a site from its URL, or its "address."

Many URLs end in *.com*, *.edu*, or *.org*. The ending *.com* is often for businesses—they want to sell something. The ending *.org* is for an organization like a charity or a political group—they usually aren't selling something, but they might have information about their activities. The ending *.edu* is almost always a school or university—they often have free educational information. Here are some examples:

- www.amazon.com: You might be able to buy something online at this site.
- www.ohio.edu: You might get free information about a university. You might get information about work that people at the university are doing.
- www.volunteermatch.org: You might get free information about a group's activities. There might also be something to buy.

13 Practicing Your Search Skills

1. Open a search engine such as Google. Use keywords to search for a school near you that teaches English.

2. Look at the URLs on the first page of your results. Do the URLs end in .com, .edu, or .org?

3. Pick one or two URLs that you think are useful. Visit the websites. Were you right? Visit one or two URLs that you don't think are useful. Were you right?

4. Print out or write down the search results. Circle the useful URLs. Bring the page to class to compare and discuss your experience.

Talk It Over

14 Interviewing Class Members

1. Work in groups of four. Write your teacher's name and the names of your group members in the spaces at the top of the chart on the following page.

2. Look at the example (Stacy).

Example
You: What are you doing this weekend?
Stacy: I'm going to visit my cousin.

3. Write your own question for the last item on the chart.

4. As a class, ask your teacher the questions and write your teacher's answers on the chart.

5. Take turns asking your three other group members the questions. Write their answers on the chart.

Question	Name	Teacher	Name	Name	Name
	Stacy	_____	_____	_____	_____
What are you doing this weekend?	Visiting my cousin				
Do you like shopping at the mall? Why or why not?	Yes. It's fun.				
Do you shop online? Why or why not?	No. I don't have a computer.				
Do you try to save money?	No				
Do you try to save energy?	Yes				
Do you try to save time?	Yes				
Your question:					

Giving Reasons

Returning Things To A Store

Sometimes you have to give a reason when you return things to a store. Some reasons are:

- "It doesn't fit."
- "It's not the right size."
- "It doesn't work."
- "It's too expensive."
- "I don't like the color."

When you return things:

- You usually need to bring your *receipt*.
- You sometimes get your money *refunded* (you get it returned).
- You sometimes get your item *exchanged* (you get a new item).
- You sometimes give the clerk your name and address.

March 23/14:14

Drawing Ink 30 ml / 95346
1 @ 1 for 10.99 MDS
                                    10.99

Pencil Toppers / 13087
1 @ 1 for 2.99 MDS
                                     2.99

Micro Pen .25MM B / 06363
1 @ 1 for 5.99 MDS
                                     5.99
****
Subtotal
Sales Tax   19.97
Total   1.59
*** 21.56
Cash
                                    21.56

If you are not completely satisfied with your purchase, simply return it with your receipt and we will gladly issue a refund.

▲ A receipt

1 **Listening for Reasons** Listen to the conversation and answer this question.

What is the woman returning? Circle the number of the correct photo.

▲ Photo 1

▲ Photo 2

2 **Listening for Specific Information** Listen to the conversation again. Choose the best answer to each question.

1. Why is the customer returning the sweater?
   - Ⓐ It's too expensive.
   - Ⓑ It's not the right size.
   - Ⓒ She doesn't like the color.

2. What does the customer give the clerk?
   - Ⓐ money
   - Ⓑ her telephone number
   - Ⓒ a receipt

3. How much is the sweater?
   - Ⓐ $43.99
   - Ⓑ $45.99
   - Ⓒ $43.95

3 **Discussing Reasons** Look at these two lists. On the left are items you can buy at a store. On the right are possible reasons to return the items. Match the items with the reasons. There may be more than one reason for each item.

Item		Reasons
1. shoes	_d, f, g_	a. It doesn't work.
2. purse	_____	b. It was a gift. I already have one.
3. calculator	_____	c. It was a gift. I don't like this music.
4. TV	_____	d. It's/They're too small.
5. shirt	_____	e. It's/They're too big.
6. radio	_____	f. I don't like the style.
7. CD	_____	g. I don't like the color.

4 **Giving Reasons** Practice giving reasons with a partner. Use the two lists in Activity 3.

Example

A: May I help you?

B: Yes. I'd like to return this _____.
                                          (item)

A: Why are you returning the _____?
                                          (item)

B: Because _____.
                        (reason)

_____

_____

5 **Role-Play** Work with a partner. Student A is a clerk in a store. Student B is a customer. The customer is returning an item to the store.

1. The store clerk asks the customer questions and completes the Return Form below.

2. The customer chooses an item and gives a reason for returning it. You can use the list of items in Activity 3 on page 38, or you can use your own ideas. (Note: You don't have to give your real address.)

RETURN FORM

Customer's name: _____

Customer's address: _____

Items returned: _____

Reason for return: _____

Cash refunded: _____

Clerk's signature: _____

Aplus Merchandise Stores Inc. • 227 Cedar Avenue • Springfield • CA • 90028

PART 3 Listening

Getting Meaning from Context

1 **Using Context Clues** Beth, Alicia, and Ali are window-shopping at a large shopping mall. You will hear five conversations with Beth, Alicia, and Ali. Listen to each conversation. Write the number of the conversation next to the place. Continue to listen to check each answer.

_____ a clothing store

_____ a bookstore

_____ a sporting goods store

___1___ an ATM (automated teller machine)

_____ a bakery

Alicia, Beth, and Ali ▶
shopping at a mall

Before You Listen

2 Preparing to Listen Before you listen, discuss these questions with a partner.

1. Do you ever wear blue jeans? When?
2. What kind (brand) of jeans do you like?
3. Where do you buy jeans?
4. How much do jeans usually cost?

A pair of jeans ▶

3 Vocabulary Preview Listen to these words and expressions. Check (✓) the words and expressions that you don't know.

Noun	Adjective	Expressions
▪ brand	▪ favorite	▪ a pair of (jeans)
		▪ on sale
		▪ the best deal
		▪ the lowest/best/highest price

Listen

4 Listening for the Main Idea You are going to listen to three ads for blue jeans. As you listen, answer this question.

1. What kind of jeans are they? Check (✓) the correct answer.

_____ Western Wonders

_____ Wild West

_____ Wild and Wooly

5 **Listening for Store Names** Listen again. Draw a line to match the ad number to the store name.

1. Ad 1   a.

2. Ad 2   b.

LARSON'S
DISCOUNT HOUSE

3. Ad 3   c.

COST $ CLUB

6 **Listening for Prices** Listen again. Draw a line to match the price of the jeans to the store.

1. $31.99   a.

Morton's
DEPARTMENT STORE

2. $35.99   b.

LARSON'S
DISCOUNT HOUSE

3. $29.99   c.

COST
$CLUB

7 Listening to Compare Prices Listen to the ads again. Then answer these questions with a partner.

1. Which store has the highest price for Wild West jeans?
2. Where is the best place to buy Wild West jeans? Why?

After You Listen

8 Comparing Prices and Stores Talk about the answers to these questions in small groups.

1. Where do you usually buy clothes?
2. Which store in your city or town has the best prices for clothes?

Listening to Online Shopping Information

Before You Listen

9 Preparing to Listen Before you listen, talk about the Internet with a partner.

1. What kind of websites do you like?
2. What kinds of websites do you visit or use often?

10 Vocabulary Preview Listen to these words and phrases. Check (✓) the ones that you don't know.

Nouns
- ■ furniture
- ■ gift
- ■ groceries*
- ■ online shopper

- ■ purchase
- ■ shipping
- ■ transaction

Verbs
- ■ deliver
- ■ fill out (a form)
- ■ place an order
- ■ promise

* This noun is always plural.

Listen

11 Listening for the Main Idea Now listen to the information. As you listen, answer this question.

What kind of website is SuperMall22.com?

12 Listening to Online Shopping Information Listen again. This time, listen for the answers to these questions.

1. In what two ways is SuperMall22.com different from other shopping websites?

First way: _____

Second way: _____

2. What kinds of things can you buy at SuperMall22.com? List three:

_____

_____

_____

3. You order something from SuperMall22.com at 1 P.M. on Tuesday. You receive it at (circle the correct time):

a. 5 P.M. on Tuesday   **b.** 1 P.M. on Wednesday   **c.** 2 P.M. on Tuesday

4. How does SuperMall22.com save time?

_____

_____

After You Listen

13 Discussing Online Shopping Answer these questions in small groups.

1. What are some advantages (good things) of online shopping? What are some disadvantages (bad things)?

2. Do you use shopping websites? Why or why not?

3. Do you think shopping online will be different in the future? How?

Talking About Clothes

1 **Identifying Clothing** Look at the words in the box. Then look at the photos. Write the name of each item of clothing under the correct photo.

baseball cap	dress	pants	shorts
blouse	jacket	shirt	sweater
boots	jeans	shoes	sweatshirt

1. _____

2. _____

3. _____

4. _____

5. _____

6. _____

7. _____

8. _____

9. _____

10. _____

11. _____

12. _____

2 Asking About Clothes Look at the photo of Vanessa. Ask your teacher if you don't know the name or color of an item of clothing that you see. Write a description in the boxes. Now look around the classroom. Ask your teacher if you don't know the name or color of any item of clothing that you see.

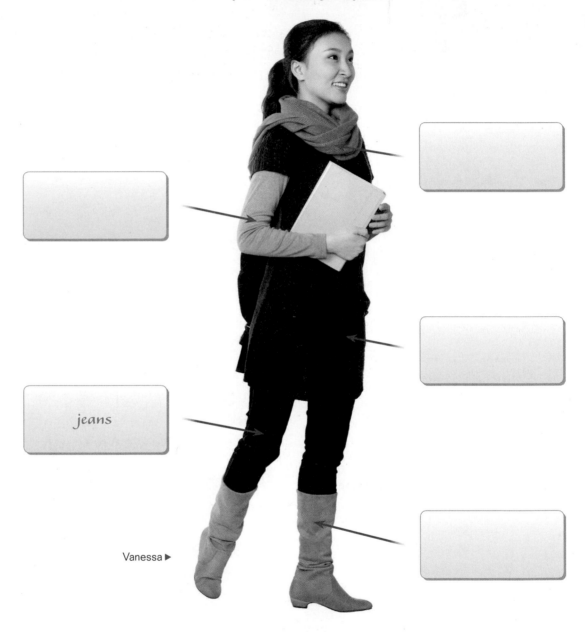

jeans

Vanessa ▶

3 Describing Clothes Describe the clothes someone in class is wearing. Don't say which person you are talking about. Use color in your description. Let the class guess whom you are describing. The first person to guess correctly takes the next turn. Continue until everyone has a turn.

4 **Asking About Prices** Work in groups of three. Each person chooses a different letter: A, B, or C. Student A looks at the Morton's Department Store ad on this page; Student B looks at the Larson's Discount House ad on page 48; Student C looks at the Cost Club ad on page 48. Ask your partners about the prices for items at the store ad they are looking at and write the prices in the spaces below. Do NOT look at your partners' ads!

1. How much are Wild West blue jeans

   at Morton's? $ _____

   at Larson's? $ _____

   at Cost Club? $ _____

2. How much are Sun Ban sunglasses

   at Morton's? $ _____

   at Larson's? $ _____

   at Cost Club? $ _____

3. How much are Spring Step aerobic shoes

   at Morton's? $ _____

   at Larson's? $ _____

   at Cost Club? $ _____

Student A

Student B

Student C

5 **Comparing Prices** Answer these questions about the three advertisements in your groups.

1. Where is the best place to buy Wild West blue jeans? Why?
2. Where is the best place to buy Sun Ban sunglasses? Why?
3. Where is the best place to buy Spring Step aerobic shoes? Why?
4. Where do you buy blue jeans, sunglasses, and aerobic shoes in your community? Why?

Self-Assessment Log

Check (✓) the words and expressions that you learned in this chapter.

Nouns	Verbs	Adjectives
▨ brand	▨ browse	▨ crowded
▨ furniture	▨ deliver	▨ favorite
▨ gift	▨ fill out (a form)	
▨ groceries	▨ look around	**Expressions**
▨ mall	▨ look for (parking)	▨ a pair of (jeans)
▨ online shopper	▨ place an order	▨ No problem!
▨ purchase	▨ promise	▨ on sale
▨ shipping	▨ save money/time/energy/gas	▨ the best deal
▨ transaction	▨ spend money/time	▨ the lowest/best/ highest price
	▨ try (on)	

Check (✓) the things you did in this chapter. How well can you do each one?

	Very well	Fairly well	Not very well
I can listen for main ideas.	☐	☐	☐
I can listen for specific information.	☐	☐	☐
I can guess the meanings of words from context.	☐	☐	☐
I can identify and use stress and reductions.	☐	☐	☐
I can evaluate my Internet search results.	☐	☐	☐
I can give reasons for returns.	☐	☐	☐
I can listen for prices and online shopping information.	☐	☐	☐
I can use a graphic organizer to compare and contrast.	☐	☐	☐
I can talk about clothes and compare prices.	☐	☐	☐

Write about what you learned and what you did in this chapter.

In this chapter,

I learned _____

_____

I liked _____

_____

CHAPTER 3

Friends and Family

"In time of test, family is best."

Burmese Proverb

Using Language
• Starting and Ending Conversations

Listening
• Listening to Voicemail Messages
• Listening to Descriptions of People

Speaking
• Leaving Voicemail Messages
• Describing People

Connecting to the Topic

1. How are Lee, Beth, and Ali staying in touch with their friends and families?

2. What are two good things about using the Internet to stay in touch? What are two bad things?

3. How do you stay in touch with friends and family?

Staying in Touch

Before You Listen

1 Prelistening Questions (Part 1) Ask and answer these questions with a classmate.

1. Do you have friends and family in another city or country? Describe.

2. How do you stay in touch with (talk, email, text) them?

3. Which of the following do you use: texting, Skype, Facebook, email, cell phone? When and why?

2 Prelistening Questions (Part 2) Look at the picture. Lee, Beth, and Ali are in a coffee shop. Talk to a group of your classmates and answer these questions.

1. How do Beth, Lee, and Ali look? Happy? Sad? Worried?

2. Why do you think they look like this?

3. What do you think they are looking at?

3 Vocabulary Preview Listen to these words from Ali, Beth, and Lee's conversation. Check (✓) the ones that you don't know.

Nouns
- post
- social media
- text message
- updates

Verbs
- grow up
- have to

- post
- stay (keep) in touch with
- text (texting)

Adjective
- amazing

Expressions
- by email/phone
- for free
- Isn't it?
- It sure is!
- once a week
- on Facebook/Skype/ Twitter

4 **Guessing the Meanings of New Words from Context** Guess the meanings of the underlined words. Write your guesses on the lines. Check your answers with a dictionary or with your teacher.

1. I bought a new computer. The store gave me a printer <u>for free</u>. I didn't have to pay for it!

   My guess: _____

2. I call my family every Sunday. I want to call more often, but it's too expensive. I can only talk to them <u>once a week</u>.

   My guess: _____

3. I love to read <u>posts</u> on Facebook about what my friends are doing!

   My guess: _____

4. I <u>have to</u> finish my homework. I need to give it to my teacher tomorrow.

   My guess: _____

5. I can't believe how beautiful and warm the beach is. I love it! It's <u>amazing</u>!

   My guess _____

6. My sister's son gets bigger every day. I love watching him <u>grow up</u>.

   My guess: _____

7. Many websites let people write messages, share information, and connect with other people. Do you use these <u>social media</u> sites?

   My guess: _____

8. My friend moved to another city, but we still <u>keep in touch</u> by phone and email.

   My guess: _____

9. People shouldn't send messages on their phone while they are driving. <u>Texting</u> while driving is very dangerous.

   My guess: _____

10. **A:** "It's so warm and sunny today."

    B: "It's a beautiful day."

    A: "<u>It sure is</u>!"

    My guess: _____

Listen

5 **Listening for Main Ideas** Listen to the first part of the conversation. Choose the best answer to each question.

1. What is Ali doing on his computer?

   (A) playing games and listening to music

   (B) doing his homework

   (C) using social media

2. What are Beth, Ali and Lee talking about?

    Ⓐ computer games

    Ⓑ keeping in touch

    Ⓒ doing homework

3. How do Beth, Ali and Lee sound?

    Ⓐ happy

    Ⓑ sad

    Ⓒ confused

6 **Listening for Specific Information (Part 1)** Now listen to the whole conversation. Choose the best answer to each question.

1. What social media site does Ali use?

    Ⓐ Myspace

    Ⓑ Skype

    Ⓒ Facebook

2. What does he like to do on the site?

    Ⓐ post updates

    Ⓑ read posts from friends

    Ⓒ talk to his family

3. Does Ali's family use Facebook?

    Ⓐ His parents and his sister do.

    Ⓑ His parents do, but his sister doesn't.

    Ⓒ His sister does, but his parents don't.

4. What do Ali's parents use?

    Ⓐ social media and email

    Ⓑ telephone only

    Ⓒ email and telephone

5. How does Ali call his sister?

    Ⓐ with Skype on the computer

    Ⓑ with international calling on his phone

    Ⓒ on Facebook

6. Who does Ali see playing and talking online?

    Ⓐ his parents

    Ⓑ his sister

    Ⓒ his sister's baby

7 Listening for Specific Information (Part 2) Listen to the conversation again. Choose the best answer to each question.

1. Ali says, "She often posts pictures of her baby." Who is he talking about?

   - Ⓐ his mother
   - Ⓑ his friend
   - Ⓒ his sister

2. Beth says, "Do they have email?" Who is she talking about?

   - Ⓐ Ali's brother and sister
   - Ⓑ Ali's parents
   - Ⓒ Ali's friends

3. Who says, "It sure is!" and why?

   - Ⓐ Lee says it because he is agreeing with Beth.
   - Ⓑ Ali says it because he disagrees with Beth.
   - Ⓒ Beth says it because she thinks the baby is cute.

After You Listen

8 Vocabulary Review Complete these sentences. Use words from the box.

amazing	have to	posts
by email	keep in touch	social media
grow up	once a week	texting

1. My mother and father live far away. We try to _____, but it's hard.

2. I lived in Thailand when I was a child. Where did you _____?

3. I exercise _____, but I really want to exercise every day.

4. He asked me to send him the information _____, but I don't have his address.

5. My friend doesn't have a smart phone, but she does have a cell phone. We stay in touch by _____ instead of email.

6. Do you _____ go now? Please stay a little longer.

7. She goes on Facebook many times each day. She likes to see the _____ from her friends.

8. He remembers the names and email addresses of everyone in his classes. It's _____!

9. I use _____, but I don't post personal information.

Stress

9 **Listening for Stressed Words** Listen to the first part of the conversation again. The stressed words are marked.

Beth: What are you doing, Ali?

Ali: I'm on Facebook.

Lee: Are you posting something? Or just reading?

Ali: I'm reading some posts from my friends. I like to see what they are doing.

10 **Marking Stressed Words** Now listen to the rest of the conversation. This time, mark the stressed words that you hear.

Beth: I like to get updates, too. Facebook is a good way to keep in touch with friends.

Lee: Is your family on Facebook, too?

Ali: My sister is. She often posts pictures of her baby. It's fun to see him grow up. But my parents don't want to use social media.

Reductions

11 **Comparing Long and Reduced Forms** Listen to the following sentences from the conversation. How is the reduced form different? Repeat them after the speaker.

Long Form	**Reduced Form***
1. What are you doing?	What are ya doin'*?
2. I like to see what they are doing.	I like to see what they're doing.
3. They don't want to use it.	They don't wanna* use it.
4. I can call them for free.	I can call 'em* for free.
5. I am going to try that.	I'm gonna* try that.

12 **Listening for Reductions** Listen and circle the letter of the sentence that you hear.

1. **a.** What are you doing? **b.** What are ya doin'*?
2. **a.** I like to see what they are doing. **b.** I like to see what they're doing.
3. **a.** They don't want to use it. **b.** They don't wanna* use it.
4. **a.** I can call them for free. **b.** I can call 'em* for free.
5. **a.** I am going to try that. **b.** I 'm gonna* try that.

*Note that the reduced forms (*) are not correct written forms of words.

Using the Internet

Using the Internet: Researching Words

You can use Google (or other search engines) to find out how people use words and phrases. Type the word or phrase into the search bar. For example, if you put in *it sure is* you will see how people use that phrase.

Example

it sure is		Submit

Search Results

- Is it scary? *It sure is* - The Washington Monthly
  www.washingtonmonthly.com/archives/individual/.../023330.php
  Apr 13, 2010 – *It sure is,*" said tea party leader Al Gerhart of Oklahoma City,
- *It Sure Is* Monday - Wikipedia, the free encyclopedia
  en.wikipedia.org/wiki/It_Sure_Is_Monday
  "*It Sure Is* Monday" is the title of a song written by Dennis Linde and recorded by American country music artist Mark Chesnutt. It was released in May 1993 as…
- Folklore.org: Macintosh Stories: *It Sure Is* Great To Get Out Of That…
  www.folklore.org/StoryView.py?project=Macintosh&story…txt
  It took a monumental effort, fueled by inordinate amounts of chocolate covered espresso beans (see Real Artists Ship), to finally finish the first release of the…

13 Practice Researching Words Look on the Internet to see how these words and expressions are used. Write some examples of the sentences you find when you search. Answer the questions on this page and the next page.

for free	It's amazing	once a week
have to	keep in touch	

1. Search for "keep in touch" online. What are some examples of how this is used? Write at least two examples.

_____

_____

_____

2. What are some things people should do "once a week?"

_____

_____

_____

3. What are some things you can get "for free?"

_____

_____

_____

4. Write down three sentences you find with "have to."

_____

_____

_____

5. Are there songs with "it's amazing" in them? What are they about?

_____

_____

_____

6. What kinds of information can you get about words on Google (or another search engine)?

_____

_____

_____

Talk It Over

14 **Discussing Keeping in Touch** You will conduct a small group survey to find out how the people in your group keep in touch.

1. Work in groups of four. Write your teacher's name and the names of your group members in the spaces at the top of the chart on page 59.

2. Look at the example:

Example

A. Do you use email?	**A.** Do you use any social media sites?
B. Yes.	**B.** Yes.
A. Who do you email?	**A.** Which ones?
B. My parents and my friends.	**B.** Mostly Facebook...

3. As a class, practice asking your teacher the questions and write the answers in the spaces.

4. Take turns asking your group members the questions and write the answers in the chart.

Question	Name	Teacher	Name	Name	Name
	Stacy				
Do you use email? Who do you email?	Yes. My parents and friends				
Do you text message? Who do you text message? Why? Why not?	No. Too difficult				
Do you use any social media sites? Which ones?	Yes. Facebook				
Do you post messages on websites? Which ones? Why or why not?	Sometimes. Facebook. Write to my friends.				

PART 2   Using Language

Starting and Ending Conversations

FOCUS

Starting Conversations

People often start conversations with people they don't know. Sometimes this happens at a party or in a new class because you want to meet someone new. Sometimes this happens on the street because you need help or directions. Here are some expressions people use to start conversations.

- Excuse me. I don't think we've met. My name is _____.
- Hello. My name is _____.
- Hi. I'm _____. How's it going?
- Hello. How are you?
- Hey! How are you doing?
- Excuse me. May I ask you a question?
- Excuse me. Can you help me?

1 **Starting Conversations in Different Situations** Work in small groups. Think of some situations where you need to start a conversation with someone. It can be with a friend, someone you know a little, or with a stranger. Write your ideas below. Write some expressions from page 59 that you can use to start the conversation.

Situation	Expressions
Asking for directions	*Excuse me. Can you help me?*

2 **Listening for Conversation Starters** Listen to the conversations and answer this question:

Where are the speakers? Write the number of the conversation under the photo below and the photos on page 61.

_____   _____

 3 **Listening for Details** Listen to the conversations again. Choose the best answer to each question.

Conversation 1 What does the shopper buy?

- (A) a blue shirt
- (B) a green shirt
- (C) a white shirt

Conversation 2 Who is Ann?

- (A) Ben's friend
- (B) Ben's sister
- (C) Ben's mother

Conversation 3 How can the tourists get to the park?

- (A) left, and then right
- (B) straight and then left
- (C) straight and then right

Ending Conversations

Here are some expressions that end conversations. You can use them in conversation, online, or on the phone:

- Would you excuse me, please? I'm late for a meeting.
- I've got to go now. I'll talk to you later.
- Can I call you back?

- It was nice to meet you/talk to you.
- I hope to see you soon.
- Give me a call when you get a chance.

4 Greetings in Different Cultures People from different cultures or areas greet each other and end conversations in different ways. Work with a group. Discuss the examples below. Do you do any of these? Fill in the chart.

	Greeting or ending a conversation	Who or when?	Do this? Why or why not?	Where in the world do people do this?
Shake hands				
Kiss a friend on one cheek				
Kiss a friend on both cheeks				
Hug				
Bow				
Other:				

5 Relationships Look at the pictures below. Work with a partner. What do you think is the relationship between the people in the pictures? Are they friends? Family members? Strangers? Do they work together? Where are they? Compare your answers with others in the class.

a. _____

b. _____

c. _____

d. _____

e. _____

f. _____

6 **Role-Play** Work with a partner. Choose a situation from Activity 1. Prepare a dialog that includes at least one of the expressions for starting a conversation and at least one of the expressions for ending the conversation. Share your dialog with the class.

Getting Meaning from Context

1 **Using Context Clues** You will hear five conversations. Listen to each conversation and choose the best answer.

1. What is Beth doing?
   - Ⓐ writing emails to her friends
   - Ⓑ posting photos
   - Ⓒ reading messages from her friends

2. How much did Ali pay for his t-shirts?
   - Ⓐ $24
   - Ⓑ $48
   - Ⓒ $12

3. How often does Ali call his parents?
   - Ⓐ every day
   - Ⓑ once a month
   - Ⓒ once a week

4. What does Ali think about the sunset?
   - Ⓐ He doesn't like it.
   - Ⓑ He really likes it.
   - Ⓒ He can't see it.

5. What is Alicia going to get at the mall?
   - Ⓐ a present for her brother
   - Ⓑ a card for her brother
   - Ⓒ a present and a card for her brother

Before You Listen

2 Preparing to Listen Before you listen, talk about voicemail with a partner.

1. Do you use voicemail? When?
2. List all of the ways you leave messages for other people (text, voicemail, paper...)

3 Vocabulary Preview Listen to these verbs. Check (✓) the verbs that you don't know.

Verbs

- call someone back
- come by
- get together with someone
- leave a message
- look forward to something

Listen

4 Listening for the Main Idea Listen to Dan's voicemail messages and answer the question.

How many people left messages for Dan? _____

5 Listening to VoiceMail Listen again. This time, write the number of each message below the photo that matches it.

_____   _____

_____   _____

After You Listen

6 **Discussing Voicemail** In small groups, look at the following voicemail messages. Answer these questions:

1. Who do you think recorded each message?

2. Is each one for a business phone or a personal phone?

3. What do you think of these messages? Which are:

   - Formal?
   - Informal?
   - Humorous?

a. Hello, you've reached Anna Gomez. I'm out of the office right now. Please leave your name and number, and I'll call you back.

b. Hi. I'm either in class or sleeping. Or both. You know what to do.

c. Hello. You've reached the Blake residence. You can leave a message for Bob, Laura, or Benji.

d. I'm sorry. Sarah is not available right now. Please leave a message after the beep.

e. If you are a friend, leave a message. If you are selling something, go away. If you are my mother, I'll be home soon.

f. You've reached the office of Sam Chang. I am unable to take your call. Please leave your name, number, and a short message.

Create your own voicemail message. Is it for business or personal? Is it formal, informal, or humorous?

Listening to Descriptions of People

◀ Alicia

Before You Listen

7 **Preparing to Listen** Look at the picture of Alicia. With a partner, think of 3 words that describe Alicia. Share your ideas with the class.

8 **Vocabulary Preview** Listen to these adjectives. Check the ones that you don't know.

Adjectives

- casual
- curly
- friendly
- heavy
- just right
- light
- medium-sized
- perfect
- slender
- straight
- thin
- typical

Listen

 9 **Listening for the Main Idea** Listen to the description of Alicia. Answer this question:

Why is Alicia a typical college student? _____

_____

 10 **Listening to Descriptions of People** Listen again. After you listen, with a partner, try to write the words you heard in the blanks below:

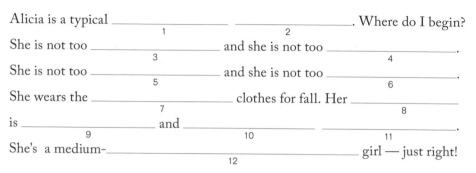

Alicia is a typical _____ _____. Where do I begin?
                          1   2
She is not too _____ and she is not too _____.
                      3   4
She is not too _____ and she is not too _____.
                      5   6
She wears the _____ clothes for fall. Her _____
                     7   8
is _____ and _____ _____.
       9   10   11
She's a medium-_____ girl — just right!
                          12

After You Listen

 11 **Discussing Appearances**
How would you describe yourself on the phone to someone you have never met? Tell your partner.

"I'm tall and I have curly brown hair. ▶
I wear casual clothes."

PART 4 Speaking

 1 **Describing People**

1. In Space 1 on page 67, draw a detailed picture of a person's face. Use at least 5 of the items from the list on the right. Check with your teacher if you don't understand a word. Don't let your partner see your drawing.

2. Describe your drawing to your partner. Your partner will draw the face you describe in Space 2.

3. Listen while your partner describes his/her picture. Draw the face your partner describes in Space 2.

4. Now compare pictures. Are the pictures the same? How and why are they different?

Space 1

Space 2

Face Shape
round
oval
square
heart-shaped

Hair
short
long
straight
curly
light
dark

Nose
large
small

Clothing
glasses
hat
casual
formal

Eyes
large
small
close-set
long eyelashes
bushy eyebrows
thin eyebrows

Mouth
large
small
smiling
frowning

Facial Hair
mustache
beard

Skin
freckles
dark skin
light skin

2 Describing a Classmate Write 5 sentences about one of your classmates. Describe the person's height, hair, eyes, and face. Write one sentence about something special about the person. Read your description to the class. Your classmates can try to guess who you are describing.

a. Height (tall, short, medium) _____

_____

b. Hair (long, short, curly, straight) _____

_____

c. Eyes (large, small, blue, black, brown, green) _____

_____

d. Face (round, oval, mustache, glasses, etc.) _____

_____

e. Something special _____

_____

3 Describing People Work with a partner. Student A has just met a new friend but can't remember the person's name. Student A describes the new friend to Student B. Student B picks the new friend from the photos. Then change roles.

▲ Paul

▲ Carly

▲ Samantha

▲ James

▲ Tamara

▲ Justin

Self-Assessment Log

Check (✓) the words and expressions that you learned in this chapter.

Nouns
- post
- social media
- text message
- updates

- look forward to something
- post
- stay/keep in touch with
- text

- perfect
- slender
- straight
- thin
- typical

Verbs
- call someone back
- come by
- get together with someone
- grow up
- have to
- leave a message

Adjectives
- amazing
- casual
- curly
- friendly
- heavy
- light
- medium-sized

Expressions
- by email/phone
- for free
- Isn't it?
- It sure is!
- once a week
- on Facebook/Skype

Check (✓) the things you did in this chapter. How well can you do each one?

	Very well	Fairly well	Not very well
I can listen for main ideas.	☐	☐	☐
I can listen for specific information.	☐	☐	☐
I can guess the meanings of words from context.	☐	☐	☐
I can identify and use stress and reductions.	☐	☐	☐
I can research new words online.	☐	☐	☐
I can start and end conversations.	☐	☐	☐
I can listen for information on voicemail.	☐	☐	☐
I can understand descriptions of people.	☐	☐	☐
I can describe people.	☐	☐	☐

Write about what you learned and what you did in this chapter.

In this chapter,

I learned _____

_____

I liked _____

_____

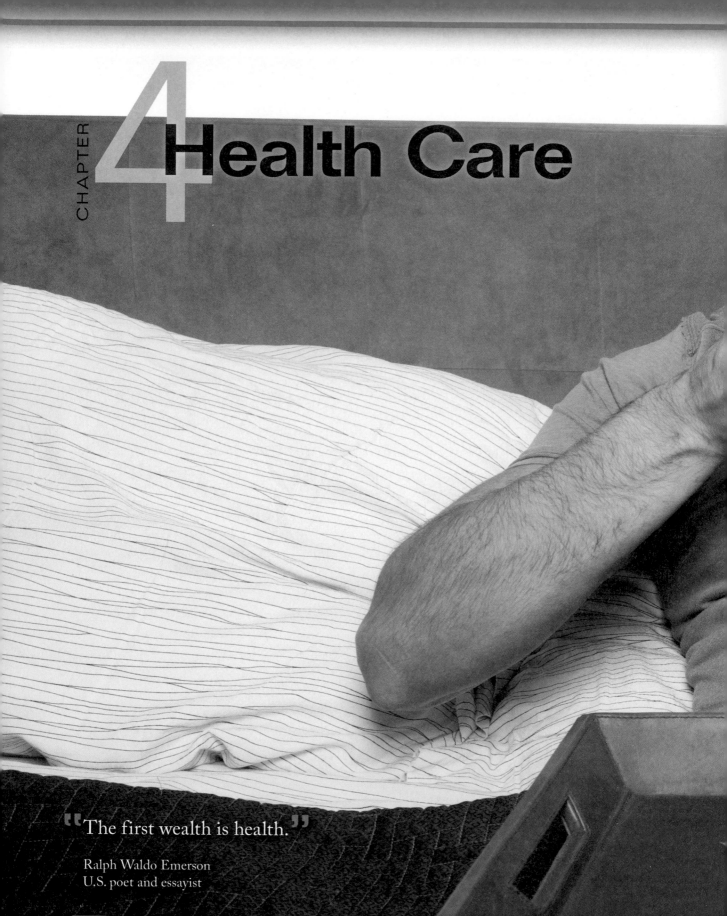

4 Health Care

"The first wealth is health."

Ralph Waldo Emerson
U.S. poet and essayist

Using Language
Giving Advice

Listening
Listening to Instructions • Listening to Complaints

Speaking
Discussing Health Advice and Habits
Talking About Body Parts

Connecting to the Topic

1. Ali is sick. What do you think is wrong with him?

2. What kinds of sicknesses can you think of? List five with your group.

3. What should you do if you have a cold? What about the flu?
   List five things for each.

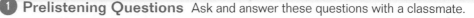

Calling a Hospital

Before You Listen

1 Prelistening Questions Ask and answer these questions with a classmate.

1. How often do you catch a cold?
2. How often do you get the flu?
3. How often do you go to a clinic or hospital to see a doctor?
4. When did you see a doctor last (most recently)?
5. Where and why did you see the doctor?
6. Does your school have a student health clinic? If yes, describe it.
7. A hospital has many services. Describe the following services:

   a. a 24-hour pharmacy (drugstore)

   b. an ER (emergency room)

   c. Family Medicine
8. What is medical insurance?
9. Why do people need medical insurance?
10. What kind of insurance do you have (e.g., car, medical, home, life)?

Look at the photos below and answer the questions on page 73 with your classmate.

Photo 1 ▶

COUGH MEDICINE

INDICATIONS:
Temporarily relieves cough due to minor throat and bronchial irritation as may occur with a cold.

DIRECTIONS:
Do not take more than 8 capsules in any 24-hour period.

ADULTS AND CHILDREN 12 YEARS AND OVER: Take 2 capsules every 6 to 8 hours, as needed.

CHILDREN UNDER 12 YEARS: Ask a doctor. Store at 68–77°F (20–25°C). Avoid excessive heat above 104°F (40°C). Protect from light.

◀ Photo 2

1. What do you think is wrong with the man in Photo 1?
2. What type of medication do you think the man in Photo 1 is taking?
3. What do you think the young woman in Photo 2 is asking the man at the counter?
4. What is the young woman in Photo 2 doing?
5. Where do you think the young woman in Photo 2 is?
6. Do you think the man in Photo 1 should see a doctor? Why or why not?

2 **Vocabulary Preview** Ali is calling the Faber Hospital health clinic. Listen to these words and expressions from Ali's conversation. Check (✓) the ones that you don't know.

Nouns
- emergency
- (the) flu
- health clinic
- ID card
- insurance card/ insurance number
- menu options

Verbs
- hang up
- make an appointment
- press
- stay on the line

3 **Guessing the Meanings of New Words from Context** Guess the meanings of the underlined words. Write your guesses on the lines. Check your answers with a dictionary or with your teacher.

1. You can't walk into a doctor's office to see the doctor at any time that you want. You have to see the doctor on a specific day, so you have to <u>make an appointment</u> first.

   My guess: _____

2. The university has a <u>health clinic</u>; all the students go there when they are sick.

   My guess: _____

3. When Ali came to the university, he got an <u>ID card</u> with his name, address, photo, and student number on it.

   My guess: _____

4. Ali has a health <u>insurance card</u>. He has to bring it every time he visits the health clinic.

   My guess: _____

5. I feel sick: I'm hot and I ache all over. I think I have <u>the flu</u>.

   My guess: _____

6. If this call is an <u>emergency</u>, please call 9-1-1. The 9-1-1 operator will help you or send someone to you quickly.

   My guess: _____

7. Please <u>stay on the line</u> and wait to talk to an operator.

   My guess: _____

8. Listen to the <u>menu options</u> before choosing a number. For the pharmacy, press 1.

   My guess: _____

9. <u>Press</u> or say "zero" for the operator.

My guess: _____

10. When you finish your phone call, please don't forget to <u>hang up</u>.

My guess: _____

4 **Listening for Main Ideas (Part 1)** Listen to the first part of Ali's phone call. Choose the best answer to each question.

1. What is Ali listening to at first?

   (A) the hospital menu options

   (B) the hospital operator

   (C) the clinic doctor

2. If this were an emergency, what should Ali do?

   (A) Press "1."

   (B) Hang up and call 9-1-1.

   (C) Call the health clinic.

3. Who does Ali talk to?

   (A) someone at the pharmacy

   (B) someone in Family Medicine

   (C) someone at the health clinic

5 **Listening for Main Ideas (Part 2)** Now listen to the whole phone call. Choose the best answer to each question.

1. What does Ali do after he listens to the menu options?

   (A) He presses "1" for the 24-hour pharmacy.

   (B) He presses "2" for Family Medicine.

   (C) He presses "3" for the health clinic.

2. Why is Ali calling the health clinic?

   (A) He thinks he has the flu.

   (B) He wants to make an appointment to see a doctor.

   (C) both a and b

3. What should Ali bring to the appointment?

   (A) his student ID and health insurance card

   (B) some money

   (C) both a and b

6 **Listening for Specific Information** Listen to Ali's phone call again. Choose the best answer to each question.

1. When is Ali's appointment?
   - (A) this afternoon at one o'clock
   - (B) tomorrow afternoon at one o'clock
   - (C) the day after tomorrow at one o'clock

2. Ali says, "I'd like to see a doctor." What does the clinic receptionist say?
   - (A) "All right. Come in tomorrow afternoon at one o'clock."
   - (B) "All right. You should come in tomorrow afternoon at one o'clock."
   - (C) "All right. Could you come in tomorrow afternoon at one o'clock?"

3. At the end of the conversation, what else does the clinic receptionist remind Ali to bring?
   - (A) his ID card
   - (B) his health insurance card
   - (C) money

After You Listen

7 **Vocabulary Review** Complete the sentences below. Use the words from the box.

emergency	insurance card	to hang up
health clinic	menu options	to make an appointment
ID card	stay on the line	the flu

1. Ali's very sick. He may have _____ _____ or a cold.

2. Ali wants _ _____ to see a doctor tomorrow.

3. Here is my _____. It shows my name and address.

4. He's sick. He's going to the _____.

5. He's going to need his health __ _____ when he goes to the clinic.

6. Ali doesn't need to call 9-1-1 because it's not a/an _____.

7. Listen carefully to the _____ before choosing a number.

8. No one is answering the phone; I'm going _____ and try to call again.

9. If you need to speak to the operator, press "0" or just _____ _____.

Stress

8 Listening for Stressed Words Listen to the first part of the conversation again. Some of the stressed words are missing. Fill in the blanks with words from the box. Some words may be used more than once.

afternoon	card	ID	No	tomorrow
appointment	doctor	insurance	Oh	Would
awful	flu	like	one o'clock	
bring	help	money	think	

Receptionist: Health Clinic. Can I _____ you? ₁

Ali: Yes. I _____ I have the _____.
₂ ₃
I feel _____.
₄

Receptionist: _____ you _____ to make
₅ ₆
an _____?
₇

Ali: Yes, I'd _____ to see a _____.
₈ ₉

Receptionist: All right. Could you come in _____
₁₀
_____ at _____?
₁₁ ₁₂

Ali: Yes, I can come then. _____! Should I
₁₃
_____ any _____?
₁₄ ₁₅

Receptionist: _____ —just your _____ and
₁₆ ₁₇
_____ _____.
₁₈ ₁₉

Now read the conversation with a partner. Practice stressing words.

Reductions

9 Comparing Long and Reduced Forms Listen to the sentences from the conversation. Repeat them after the speaker. Note that the reduced forms (*) are not correct written forms of words.

Long Form

1. <u>Can</u> I help you?

2. <u>Would you</u> like to make an appointment?

3. <u>Could you</u> come in tomorrow afternoon at one?

4. No—<u>just your</u> ID <u>and</u> insurance card.

Reduced Form

1. <u>C'n*</u> I help you?

2. <u>Wudja*</u> like to make an appointment?

3. <u>Cudja*</u> come in tomorrow afternoon at one?

4. No—<u>justcher*</u> ID <u>'n*</u> insurance card.

10 Listening for Reductions Listen and then circle the letter of the sentence that you hear. Note that the reduced forms (*) are not the correct written forms of words.

1. **a.** Can I help you?
   b. C'n* I help you?

2. **a.** Would you like to make an appointment?
   b. Wudja* like to make an appointment?

3. **a.** Could you come in tomorrow afternoon at one?
   b. Cudja* come in tomorrow afternoon at one?

4. **a.** No—just your ID and insurance card.
   b. No—justcher* ID 'n* insurance card.

* Note that the reduced forms (*) are not correct written forms of words.

Using the Internet

Pronunciation Dictionaries
You can use the Internet to find out how to pronounce words. Try using the keywords *pronouncing dictionary* or *pronunciation dictionary*. Combine these with the keyword *English* to limit your results. Remember to look at the URL. The URL can tell you if the website will be useful.

11 Practicing Your Search Skills Look on the Internet for an English pronunciation dictionary. Remember to combine keywords and to check the URLs. Use the pronunciation dictionary to practice pronouncing the words in the box from this chapter.

appointment	emergency	insurance
clinic	headache	thermometer

Discuss your results with the class.

1. What keyword combinations did you use?
2. Did you check the URLs before you went to each site?
3. What is the best pronunciation dictionary on the Internet?
4. What kind of online language program would be helpful to you?

12 Discussing Solutions to Health Problems Look at the problems in the left column of the chart. Write your solution for each problem in the chart. Then, talk about what to do with your partner. Do you agree with each other? If not, why not? Write your partner's solutions in the chart.

	Your Solution	Your Partner's Solution
You have a bad headache.		
You accidentally eat or drink something bad.		
You are very sad and upset.		
You cut yourself badly.		
You have a bad toothache.		
There's a fire in your apartment.		

Giving Advice

FOCUS

Using Modals To Give Advice

Sometimes people tell you their problems and you want to give advice. To do this, you can use modals such as *could*, *might*, *should*, and *have to*. Use *have to* for a very strong suggestion. *Should* is a little less strong. Use *could* and *might* when you don't want to give strong advice.

Giving Advice		
Modal	**Meaning**	**Problem: "I'm homesick."**
could might should have to	least strong ↓ strongest	You **could** call your family. You **should** call your family. You **have to** call your family.

Before You Listen

1 **Vocabulary Preview** Rick is giving Ramona advice. Listen to these words and expressions from their conversation. Check (✓) the ones that you don't know.

Nouns
- argument
- friends

Adjective
- angry

◄ "What should I do?"

Listen

2 **Listening for Main Ideas** Listen to the conversation and answer these questions with a partner.

1. What is Ramona's problem?
2. What is Rick's advice?

3 **Listening for Specific Information** Listen to the conversation again. Choose the best answer to each question.

1. What happened to Ramona?
   - (A) She had an argument with Sue.
   - (B) She has a new friend named Sue.
   - (C) She had a party with Sue.

2. What does Rick say Sue probably feels?
   - (A) She's happy.
   - (B) She's sad.
   - (C) She's angry.

3. What advice does Rick give?
   - (A) Call Sue first, then send a letter.
   - (B) Send Sue a letter, and then call.
   - (C) Call Sue and send a letter today.

After You Listen

4 **Giving Advice** With a partner, take turns giving advice. The student who has a problem can choose from the list of problems or make up his or her own. The student who gives advice can use the advice expressions.

Problems

My neighbors are noisy. I can't sleep.

I miss my family and friends at home.

I'm afraid to speak English outside of class.

My roommate/boyfriend/girlfriend watches TV all the time.

I never have enough money.

Advice

You should _____

You could _____

You might _____

You have to _____

You don't have to _____

5 Role-Play With a partner, role-play one of the problems from Activity 4 for the class. Then, listen to other students' role-plays and answer the questions in the chart.

Questions	Role-Play 1	Role-Play 2
What was the problem?		
What was the advice?		
Do you agree with the advice?		
If you don't agree, what advice would you give?		

PART **3** Listening

Getting Meaning from Context

1 Vocabulary Preview You are going to hear some telephone calls. Listen to these words and expressions from the telephone calls. Check (✓) the ones that you don't know.

◄ "I've got a really bad headache."

Nouns
■ cavity
■ (dental) cleaning
■ checkup
■ (eye) exam

Verb
■ take your temperature

Adjective
■ stolen

2 **Using Context Clues** Here is a list of services that you can call when you need help. Read the list of services in the box and make sure that you understand each one.

> the dental clinic   the fire department   the police department
> the eye clinic   the health clinic

1. You will hear five telephone calls. The first part of each call is missing.

2. Listen to the question for each call: Who is the speaker calling? Write the number of each call in the blanks below.

_____ the health clinic   _____ the police department

_____ the dental clinic   _____ the eye clinic

_____ the fire department

3. Continue to listen to check your answers.

Listening to Instructions

Before You Listen

3 **Preparing to Listen** Before you listen, talk about illnesses with a partner.

1. Do you ever get sick?

2. What do you do when you are sick?

4 **Vocabulary Preview** You are going to hear a conversation at a health clinic. Listen to these words from the conversation. Check (✓) the ones that you don't know.

Nouns

▨ aspirin   ▨ medicine
▨ (a) cold   ▨ prescription
▨ drugstore
▨ fever   **Verbs**
▨ flu   ▨ ache
▨ fluids   ▨ cough
                   ▨ sneeze

▲ Listening to instructions at a clinic

Listen

5 **Listening for the Main Idea** Ali is at the health clinic. Listen to the conversation and answer this question.

What's wrong with Ali?

6 **Listening to Instructions** Listen again. This time, look at each photo. Listen to the doctor's advice. Cross out the incorrect words in the sentence next to each photo.

1. You should (~~go to school~~/stay in bed) and (exercise/rest) as much as possible.

2. You can take (two aspirin/four aspirin) (four times/two times) a day. That will help the fever and the aches and pains.

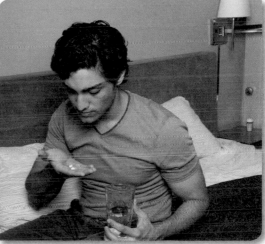

3. Be sure to (drink plenty of fluids/eat plenty of fruits). Fruit juice and (coffee/hot tea) are the best.

4. Here's a prescription for some (cold/cough) medicine. You can take it to any (department store/drugstore).

5. Be sure to take your medicine (when you feel bad/with your meals) because it might (upset your stomach/upset your mother).

Listen again and check your answers.

After You Listen

7 Discussing Your Opinion Answer these questions in small groups.

1. Talk about home remedies (things that you make at home to make you feel better). Do you use any home remedies when you get sick?

2. In your opinion, do herbal remedies (remedies that come from plants) work very well for colds and the flu? Which ones work? How do they help?

Before You Listen

8 **Preparing to Listen** You are going to hear several people explain different complaints. Before you listen, discuss this question with a classmate.

What illnesses and other problems can cause pain?

9 **Vocabulary Preview** Listen to these words and phrases. Check (✓) the ones that you don't know.

Nouns	Verbs	Expression
▪ ankle	▪ break (a leg)	▪ (an illness) is going around
▪ bandage	▪ sprain (an ankle)	
▪ headache	▪ vomit	

Listen

10 **Listening for Main Ideas** Listen to the complaints and answer these questions.

1. How many speakers do we hear? _____

2. How many speakers say that they are in pain? _____

3. What kind of pain do they have? _____

_____

_____

11 **Listening for Specific Information** Listen to the complaints again. This time, choose one of the following statements as advice for each speaker. Write the number of the speaker next to the best advice for that speaker's complaint.

_____ You should take two aspirin for the pain and see a dentist as soon as possible.

_____ You should wrap a tight bandage around your ankle. Don't walk on it for a few days.

_____ You can take some medicine from the drugstore for the sneezing and coughing. Drink plenty of fluids and try to rest.

_____ You should take two aspirin. See a doctor if your head still hurts tomorrow.

_____ You should go to a doctor and get an X-ray.

_____ You shouldn't eat anything for two or three hours—until you stop vomiting. Then you can have clear fluids. If that doesn't work, see a doctor.

After You Listen

12 **Discussing Complaints** Discuss the complaints in Activity 11 with a partner. Compare your answers. Did you both choose the same advice for each complaint? What are some other remedies for each complaint?

PART 4 Speaking

Discussing Health Advice and Habits

1 **Discussing Health Advice** Work in small groups. Answer these questions.

1. What do you do when you have a cold?
2. What special foods do you eat? What special drinks do you have?
3. What advice does your mother give you?

Share your answers with the class. Do the other students do different things when they have colds? What is the best advice?

2 **Role-Play** With a partner, role-play a conversation between a patient and a doctor. Student A is the patient; Student B is the doctor. The patient has a cold or the flu; the doctor gives advice. Then change roles.

3 **Asking About Health Habits** How healthy are the students in your class? You are going to do a health survey to find out. Work in small groups. Ask the students in your group the questions in the chart. For Questions 1 through 5, put a check (✓) in the chart for each *Yes* or *No* answer. For Question 6, write the answers in the space provided. Don't write down the students' names.

Questions	Yes	No
1. Do you exercise or play a sport?		
2. Are you at the right weight?		
3. Do you smoke?		
4. Do you get at least eight hours of sleep every night?		
5. Do you eat fruits and vegetables every day?		
6. What is your biggest health worry?		

As a class, talk about the answers to the questions. Is your class healthy?

4 **Identifying Body Parts** Work with a partner to identify these parts of the body on the photo of Lee below.

ankle	elbow	head	stomach
arm	eyes	knee	thigh
back	finger	leg	toe
cheeks	foot (feet)	neck	waist
chest	~~forehead~~	nose	wrist
chin	hair	shin	
ear	hand	shoulder	

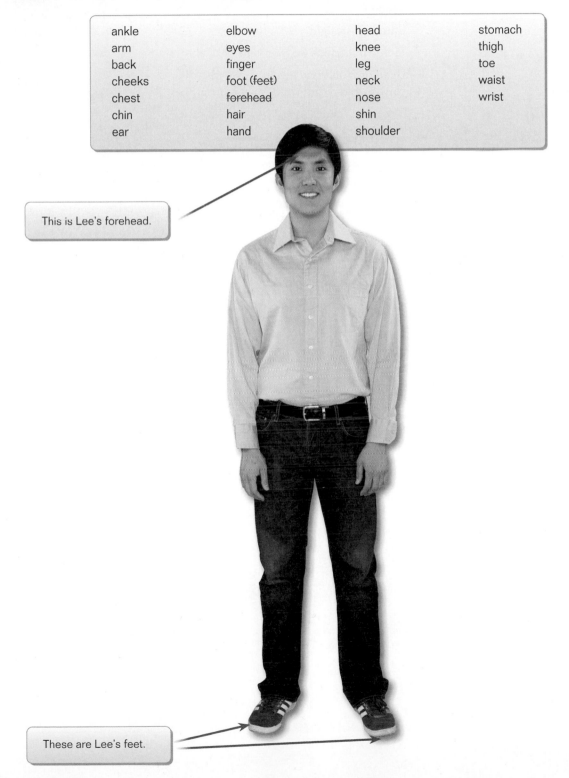

This is Lee's forehead.

These are Lee's feet.

5 **Teaching an Exercise** Think of an exercise to teach the class. Tell the class how to do your exercise. The class follows your instructions and does each exercise.

Example

Stand up straight.

Hold your hands up over your head.

Bend over and touch your toes with your fingers; bend your knees a little.

Repeat ten times.

▲ Bend and stretch to the right.

6 **Researching and Discussing Exercise** Do people exercise more or less than they did 40 years ago? Use your Internet search skills to research the questions in the chart. Fill in the chart. Then, share your answers with the class.

	Today	40 Years Ago
What do/did people do for exercise?		
Are/Were people interested in exercise?		
What sports do/did people play?		
What sports do/did people watch?		

Self-Assessment Log

Check (✓) the words and expressions that you learned in this chapter.

Nouns
- ankle
- argument
- aspirin
- bandage
- cavity
- checkup
- (a) cold
- (dental) cleaning
- drugstore
- emergency
- (eye) exam
- fever
- flu
- fluids
- friends
- headache
- health clinic
- ID card
- insurance card/ insurance number
- medicine
- menu options
- prescription

Verbs
- ache
- break (a leg)
- cough
- hang up
- make an appointment
- press
- sneeze
- sprain (an ankle)
- stay on the line
- take your temperature
- vomit

Adjectives
- angry
- stolen

Expression
- (an illness) is going around

Check (✓) the things you did in this chapter. How well can you do each one?

	Very well	Fairly well	Not very well
I can listen for main ideas.	☐	☐	☐
I can listen for specific information.	☐	☐	☐
I can guess the meanings of words from context.	☐	☐	☐
I can identify and use stress and reductions.	☐	☐	☐
I can understand health complaints and doctor's instructions.	☐	☐	☐
I can give advice using modals.	☐	☐	☐
I can search for pronounciation dictionaries on the Internet.	☐	☐	☐
I can talk about health and habits.	☐	☐	☐

Write about what you learned and what you did in this chapter.

In this chapter,

I learned _____

_____

I liked _____

_____

5 Men and Women

"What's the difference between offline friends and online friends?"

Charlie Gilkey
blogger

In this **CHAPTER**

Conversation
Making Small Talk

Listening
Listening to Invitations • Listening to Responses

Speaking
Invitations and Celebrations

Connecting to the Topic

1. Look at the people in the photo. Who are they? What are they doing?

2. What do you use the Internet for? List all the things.

3. Look at the quote. What is your answer to this question?

Making Connections at School

Before You Listen

1 **Discussing Campus Life** Look at the photos. Talk with a classmate. Describe each picture. Then, answer the questions.

1. Match these descriptions to the photo. Write the number of the photo:

   a. Students playing sports on campus   Photo _____

   b. A student newspaper   Photo _____

   c. Student volunteer group   Photo _____

   d. The Facebook page of a student club   Photo _____

2. How do the groups and activities in the photos help students to make connections (that is, to meet people) on campus?

3. What kinds of groups and activities would you like to join?

Photo 1 ▼

▲ Photo 3

▲ Photo 2

▲ Photo 4

FABER COLLEGE JOURNAL

Faber Soccer Team Goes to Finals

2 Vocabulary Preview Listen to these words and expressions from a webcast. Check (✓) the words and expressions that you don't know.

Nouns	Verbs	Adjective	Expressions
▦ exchange	▦ join	▦ intramural	▦ around the world
▦ member	▦ make connections		▦ once
▦ team	▦ practice		▦ twice
	▦ sound like		

3 Guessing the Meanings of New Words from Context Guess the meanings of the underlined words. Write your guesses on the lines. Check your answers with a dictionary or your teacher.

1. A soccer <u>team</u> has eleven players and a baseball <u>team</u> has nine players.

   My guess: _____

2. I need to change some dollars into Euros, so I'm going to a money <u>exchange</u>.

   My guess: _____

3. Facebook is really popular. There are millions of <u>members</u>.

   My guess: _____

4. School is a great place to make new friends. Students can <u>make connections</u> both in class and outside of class.

   My guess: _____

5. Sometimes, when you want to <u>join</u> a club, you have to pay some money first.

   My guess: _____

6. **A**: I'm going to the beach this weekend.

   B: That <u>sounds like</u> fun!

   My guess: _____

7. Alicia is learning the piano, so she <u>practices</u> one or two hours every day.

   My guess: _____

8. Students who want to play a sport with students in the same school can play an <u>intramural</u> sport.

   My guess: _____

9. After Beth finishes school, she wants to travel <u>around the world</u> and see all the countries.

   My guess: _____

10. Lee doesn't play sports every day. He only has time to play <u>once</u> or <u>twice</u> a week.

    My guess: _____

4 **Listening for Main Ideas (Part 1)** Listen to the first part of the webcast and choose the best answer to each question.

1. What is Alex talking about on the webcast today?
   - Ⓐ Ali, Beth, and Lee
   - Ⓑ making connections on campus
   - Ⓒ playing sports

2. Who joined a student club?
   - Ⓐ Ali and Beth
   - Ⓑ Ali and Lee
   - Ⓒ Ali, Beth, and Lee

5 **Listening for Main Ideas (Part 2)**
Listen to the complete webcast and choose the best answer to each question.

1. What does Alex think of clubs?
   - Ⓐ They are a good way to exercise.
   - Ⓑ They are a good way to meet people.
   - Ⓒ They are a good way to practice a language.

2. At the end of the webcast, what does Alex want Faber College students to remember?
   - Ⓐ to exercise
   - Ⓑ to listen to his webcast
   - Ⓒ to join a club or group

6 **Listening for Specific Information**
Listen to the complete webcast again. Choose the best answer to each question.

1. Who is learning dances from around the world and why?
   - Ⓐ Lee is because he's playing intramural soccer.
   - Ⓑ Beth and Michel are because they're in the Language Exchange Club.
   - Ⓒ Ali because he's in the International Dance Club.

2. What did Lee join?
   - Ⓐ an intramural soccer team
   - Ⓑ the Faber College basketball team
   - Ⓒ the International Dance Club

3. Where did Beth meet Michel?

   (A) in an intramural sport

   (B) in the International Dance Club

   (C) in the Language Exchange Club

4. What does Beth do with Michel in the Language Exchange Club?

   (A) She helps him with French.

   (B) She helps him with English.

   (C) She'd rather not say.

After You Listen

7 **Vocabulary Review** Complete the conversation. Use words from the box. Then, with a classmate, repeat the dialog. Pay attention to your stress and intonation.

around the world	intramural	once	team
connect	join	practice	twice
exchange	members	sounds like	

Beth: So, Lee, are you playing on the Faber College soccer _____?

Lee: No, I'm not that good!... but I am playing _____ _____ soccer.

   I really like it!

Beth: Yes, it _____ _____ fun!

Lee: And what about you, Beth? Are you going to _____ a club?

Beth: Yes, I already did! I'm in the Language _____ _____ Club.

Lee: So, what do club _____ _____ do?

Beth: We _____ foreign languages; in my case, French.

Lee: That's great! How often do you meet? Every day?

Beth: No, I wish! I can meet only _____ or _____ a week.

Lee: Still, that's a great way to meet people from _____ _____, right?

Beth: It sure is! There are members from 10 different countries... You know, Lee, we're lucky to be at Faber College: it's easy for students here to _____ with other students.

Lee: Yes, it sure is!

Stress

8 **Listening for Stressed Words** Listen to the first part of the webcast again. Some of the stressed words are missing. Fill in the blanks with words from the box. Use one of the words twice.

campus	making	students	webcast
Hi	My	Today	weeks
introduce	see	too	Welcome

Alex: _____ to another Faber College
1
_____! _____ name is Alex.
2   3
_____, we're talking about _____
4   5
connections on _____. Let me _____
6   7
three _____ we met a few _____
8   9
ago: Beth…

Beth: _____, Alex
10

Alex: Ali…

Ali: Nice to _____ you again!
11

Alex: You, _____!… and Lee.
12

Lee: _____, Alex!
13

Reductions

Reductions with *Did You*

The words *did you* reduce to /ja/ or /ju/ after *What, Where, When, Who, Why,* and *How.*

Long Form	Reduced Form
How <u>did you</u> and Beth meet?	How <u>ju</u>* and Beth meet?

9 **Comparing Long and Reduced Forms** Listen to these sentences.

Long Form	**Reduced Form**
1. How <u>did you</u> and Beth meet?	How <u>ju</u>* and Beth meet?
2. Where <u>did you</u> go last night?	Where <u>ja</u>* go last night?
3. When <u>did you</u> join the soccer team?	When <u>ja</u>* join the soccer team?
4. Why <u>did you</u> join intramural soccer?	Why <u>ja</u>* join intramural soccer?
5. What <u>did you</u> do at the dance?	What <u>ja</u>* do at the dance?
6. Who <u>did you</u> meet there?	Who <u>ju</u>* meet there?

10 **Listening for Reductions** Listen and then circle the letter of the sentence you hear.

1. **a.** What did you do last weekend?   **b.** What ja* do last weekend?

2. **a.** Why did you join the Dance Club?   **b.** Why ja* join the Dance Club?

3. **a.** How did you make connections at your school?   **b.** How ja* make connections at your school?

4. **a.** Who did you meet in the Language Exchange Club?   **b.** Who ja* meet in the Language Exchange Club?

5. **a.** When did you get here?   **b.** When ju* get here?

Using the Internet

Using Google Effectively

You know that Google is a great way to find information and to make connections with people and groups. Here are some **keywords** to find information more effectively.

Information You Need	Keywords
Clubs, groups at a school	**student groups + school name (e.g., UCLA)**
Applying to schools	**international admissions + school name**
The best schools in your major	**school rankings + major (e.g., economics; engineering)**
Business contacts in your city	**chamber of commerce + city name**
Recreation in your city	**department of parks & recreation + city name**

*Note that the reduced forms (*) are not correct written forms of the words.

11 Practicing Effective Search Skills Use your search skills to answer these questions. Then, discuss what you find with your teacher and your classmates.

1. Are there any film (movie) clubs at UCLA? If so, what is the name of the club?

2. What TOEFL score do you need if you are applying to Baruch College in New York City?

3. What is the best (#1) law school in the U.S.?

4. What is the address and phone number of the San Anselmo, California, Chamber of Commerce?

5. What is the name of the biggest park in Greenwich, Connecticut?

6. Look at the image. Try to find a similar image online. What can you find out about this place?

Talk It Over

12 Meeting People Discuss ways to meet people and make friends and connections:

1. Look at the questions in the chart on page 99. Add one question.

2. Read the example (Lisa) with your class.

3. Practice asking your questions. Think about stress and contractions.

4. Walk around the room. Ask three people the questions. Write their answers in the chart.

5. Share your answers with the class.

Question	Name	Name	Name	Name
	Lisa	_____	_____	_____
What sports do (or did) you play in high school or college?	Soccer and tennis			
What clubs or groups did you join in high school or college?	My college computer club			
Did you make friends by joining a club or playing a sport? If so, how many friends did you make?	Yes, I did. I met my best friend in the computer club and I made many other friends while playing soccer and tennis.			
Is (Was) your high school or college a good place to meet people and make friends?	I made a lot of friends in high school. But now in college, I am too busy studying!			
a. (For men): Is it OK to ask a woman for a date if you meet her in a school club? Why (not)? **b.** (For women). Is it OK to ask a man for a date if you meet him in a school club? Why (not)?	Yes, it's OK. We have some of the same interests, so it will be fun.			

Making Small Talk

FOCUS

What is Small Talk?

"Small talk" is friendly talk you can use to start conversations with people you know and with people you just met. For example, you can talk about the weather.

What are good places and topics for small talk?

Here are good places and topics for small talk and ways you can start:

Place	Topic	Examples
Outside: waiting for the bus	The weather	Nice weather, isn't it? Beautiful day, isn't it? It's really hot today, isn't it? Boy, it's really cold!
Inside: waiting in line	The long line	This line is long, isn't it? This is taking forever, isn't it? I hope we don't have to wait too long!
At a party	The people	Do you know anyone here at the party? Do you know the host? Is this your first time at (host's) place?
At a restaurant, cafeteria, or fast-food place	The place and the food	Nice restaurant, isn't it? The food here is great, isn't it? Is this your first time here? Is the food good? Boy, this place is crowded, isn't it?
At a sports event, a concert, the movies, etc.	Activities related to the event	Are you a (Yankees/Brad Pitt/U2) fan? Do you like this singer? Do you like (action/romance/sci-fi) movies? I think this is going to be a great show! What do you think?

▼ Students waiting for a concert and making small talk

Before You Listen

1 **Small Talk and Short Answer Practice** Follow these steps to practice small talk:

1. Practice the small talk opening examples in the right column on page 100.

2. Ask your classmates and/or your teacher about any words you do not understand.

3. Take turns making small talk with a classmate and giving short "yes" answers to each question.

   Example: **Student 1:** Nice weather, isn't it?

   Student 2: Yes, it is!

Listen

2 **Listening to Small Talk** Listen to four short small talk conversations. Write the number of the conversation under the photo it matches. There is one extra photo. After you listen, use that extra photo to make up a conversation with your partner.

▲ Photo A
Conversation #: _____

▲ Photo B
Conversation #: _____

▲ Photo C
Conversation #: _____

▲ Photo D
Conversation #: _____

▲ Photo E
Conversation #: _____

Strategy

Making More Small Talk

After you start small talk with someone, there are several ways to continue:

- Ask the person his/her feelings about a topic
- Continue with sub-topics or related topics
- If the person seems comfortable talking to you, introduce yourself.
- If you want to continue the conversation, ask questions about the situation.

3 Practice Listen to three conversations. The conversations appear below. Ask your teacher about any words you don't understand. Then, work with a classmate and take turns repeating the conversations. Pay attention to stress and intonation.

Conversation 1: In Line at a School Cafeteria

Man: Is this the line for the sandwiches?

Woman: Yes, it is.

Man: Thanks. I'm new here. Is the cafeteria food any good?

Woman: Yeah, usually. But don't try the coffee—it's terrible!

Man: Ha ha! OK, I won't!… I'm Brad, by the way.

Woman: Hi Brad. I'm Sharon. Nice to meet you.

Man: You, too. So, do you usually have lunch in the cafeteria?

Conversation 2: In Line at a Supermarket

Woman 1: This line is so long!

Woman 2: Yes, it's taking forever.

Woman 1: … and I hate waiting in line, don't you?

Woman 2: I sure do… but it's pretty fast here, not like at the post office.

Woman 1: Right!… By the way, my name's Susan.

Woman 2: Nice to meet you, Susan. I'm Annette.

Woman 1: Nice to meet you, too. So, do you usually shop at this supermarket?

Conversation 3: At a Baseball Game

Man 1: Great day for the game, isn't it?

Man 2: It sure is!

Man 1: So, are you a Yankee's fan?

Man 2: I sure am. How about you?

Man 1: Yeah. The Yankees are my favorite team!… By the way, my name's Mark.

Man 2: Hey, Mark. I'm Scott.

Man 1: So, are you just a Yankees fan? Do you like any other teams?

4 **Practice Continuing Small Talk** With a partner, practice saying one conversation from Activity 3. Ask two more questions about the situation or a related topic.

5 **Making Your Own Small Talk** Get up and move around the classroom. Ask the questions in the left column. Write the name of a classmate who answers "yes." Then, write his/her answer(s) to the follow-up question(s).

Question	Classmate Name	Follow-Up Questions	Answer(s)
Do you like sports?		Which ones?	
Do you like movies?		Who's your favorite actor? Why do you like him/her?	
Do you like to eat out?		What's your favorite restaurant? Why do you like it?	
Do you have a hobby or something you like to do in your free time?		What is it? Why do you like it?	
Do you like music?		What kind of music do you like? Who's your favorite singer?	

PART 3 Listening

Getting Meaning from Context

1 **Vocabulary Preview** You are going to hear some conversations. Listen to these words and expressions from the conversations. Check (✓) the ones that you don't know.

Nouns	Verbs	Adjectives	Expressions
▪ major (e.g., "a business major")	▪ ask (someone) out	▪ depressed	▪ gosh
▪ partner	▪ have a good time	▪ nervous	▪ of course
		▪ upset	▪ on a date

2 **Using Context Clues** You will hear five conversations. Listen to each conversation and choose the best answer. Continue to listen to check each answer.

1. What is Michel asking Beth?
   - (A) He's asking her to read his text message.
   - (B) He's asking her to practice English with him.
   - (C) He's asking her out on a date.

2. How does Alicia probably feel about Beth going out with Michel?
   - (A) She thinks it's a bad idea.
   - (B) She thinks it's a good idea.
   - (C) She thinks Beth should just practice French with Michel.

3. What does Ali think?
   - (A) He thinks Lee is not smart.
   - (B) He thinks Lee should ask Reema to dance with him.
   - (C) He thinks Lee should ask Reema out.

4. What just happened?
   - (A) Reema asked Lee out.
   - (B) Lee asked Reema out.
   - (C) Lee and Reema went to the movies.

5. What is Dina probably going to do?
   - (A) She's going to go out with Peter after the party.
   - (B) She's going to go out with Peter next week.
   - (C) She's not going to go out with Peter.

Listening to Invitations

Before You Listen

3 **Preparing to Listen** You are going to listen to a conversation. Before you listen, talk about invitations with a partner.

1. Do you ever invite friends to your house or apartment for dinner, a movie, and/or a party?

2. Do you like indoor dinner parties or outdoor parties like barbecues and picnics? Why?

3. Do you ever invite people using the following ways? Why or why not?
   a. Text messaging
   b. Facebook
   c. Twitter
   d. A traditional card
   e. An e-vite (online invitation)

4 **Vocabulary Preview** Listen to these words and expressions. Check (✓) the ones you don't know.

Nouns	Verbs	Adjective	Expressions
▨ potluck	▨ get together	▨ glad	▨ besides
▨ present	▨ take someone		▨ enough for
▨ secret	to dinner		(2, 3,…) people
	▨ text		▨ surprise party

Listen

5 **Listening for Main Ideas** Alicia is having lunch with Lee in the college cafeteria. She is inviting Lee to a party. Listen to their conversation and answer this question.

What kind of party is it?

6 **Listening for Specific Information** Listen again. After each statement, check *True*, *False*, or *No Info (No Information)*. Then, write a detail to support your answer.

Statement	True	False	No Info	Support
Example 1: Beth is having lunch with Lee.		✓		*Alicia is having lunch with Lee.*
Example 2: Alicia is going to invite Michel to the party.			✓	*No information*
The party is for Alicia.				
Beth knows about the party.				
The party is going to be at Alicia's.				
The party is going to be this Friday afternoon.				
Lee is going to give Beth a present.				
Lee is going to bring a salad for 50 people.				
Lee is coming to the party after Beth.				
Alicia thinks Beth's age is personal information.				

Before You Listen

7 **Vocabulary Preview** Listen to these words and expressions. Check (✓) the ones that you don't know.

Nouns	Verbs	Adjective	Expressions
▣ get together	▣ come over	▣ away	▣ at least
▣ graduation	▣ hang out		▣ How about…?
▣ picnic	▣ snack on		▣ I wish I could…
▣ stuff			▣ until
▣ wedding			

8 **Preparing to Listen to Invitations** You are going to hear six sentences with people inviting, accepting invitations, and refusing invitations. First, listen to the examples. Then, listen to the six questions and statements and check (✓) the correct box.

Example 1: Can you come to my sister's wedding next month?

Example 2: Thanks so much for inviting me! I really wish I could, but I'll be away.

	Invitations		
	Inviting	Accepting	Refusing
Example	✓		
Example			✓
1.			
2.			
3.			
4.			
5.			
6.			

Listen

9 Listening for Main Ideas Listen to the four conversations with invitations. Match the conversation to the correct photo. Then, check (✓) Accept if the person accepts and Refuse if the person refuses.

Conversation #: _____

☐ Accept   ☐ Refuse

Conversation #: _____

☐ Accept   ☐ Refuse

Conversation #: _____

☐ Accept   ☐ Refuse

Conversation #: _____

☐ Accept   ☐ Refuse

10 Listening for Specific Information Listen to each conversation with a partner. What do people say when they accept? When they refuse, what reasons do they give? Discuss.

After You Listen

11 Giving, Accepting, and Refusing Invitations Work with two other classmates. Use the pictures from Activity 9 and one of your own ideas. Take turns giving, accepting, and refusing invitations.

Invitations and Celebrations

1 Discussing Celebrations Look at the pictures below. Label each photo with the name of the celebration.

Celebrations

2 Class Survey Walk around the classroom and put a check (✓) under the "Yes" column for each classmate who answered "yes" to the following four questions. Then, ask the students answering "yes" the follow-up questions. Write their answers in the boxes on the right. Then, discuss as a whole class.

Question	"Yes" Answers	Follow-up Questions	Answers
Did you attend (go to) a wedding in the last year?		Whose? What present did you give?	
Did you attend a graduation in the last year?		Whose? What present did you give?	
Did you attend a party in the last 3 or 4 weeks?		Whose? Did you bring anything?	
Did you attend a dance, concert, or sports event in the last 3 or 4 weeks?		What event? Where?	

Self-Assessment Log

Check (✓) the words and expressions that you learned in this chapter.

Nouns
- exchange
- get together
- graduation
- major (e.g.,"a business major")
- member
- partner
- picnic
- potluck
- present
- secret
- stuff
- team
- wedding

Verbs
- ask (someone) out
- come over
- get together
- hang out
- have a good time
- join
- make connections
- practice
- snack on
- take someone to dinner
- sound like
- text

Adjectives
- away
- depressed
- glad
- intramural
- nervous
- shy
- upset

Expressions
- around the world
- at least
- besides
- enough for (2, 3,…) people
- gosh

- How about…?
- I wish I could…
- of course
- on a date
- once
- surprise party
- twice
- until

Check (✓) the things you did in this chapter. How well can you do each one?

	Very well	Fairly well	Not very well
I can listen for main ideas.	☐	☐	☐
I can listen for specific information.	☐	☐	☐
I can guess the meanings of words from context.	☐	☐	☐
I can identify and use stress and reductions.	☐	☐	☐
I can understand invitations and responses.	☐	☐	☐
I can use search engines more effectively.	☐	☐	☐
I can understand and make small talk.	☐	☐	☐
I can discuss celebrations.	☐	☐	☐

Write about what you learned and what you did in this chapter.

In this chapter,

I learned _____

_____

I liked _____

_____

6

Sleep and Dreams

> " Our dreams
> are a second life. "
>
> Gérard de Nerval
> French poet

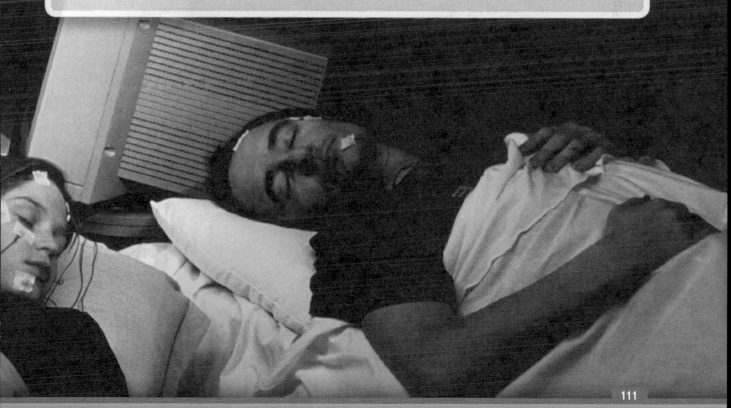

In this
CHAPTER

Using Language
Agreeing and Disagreeing

Listening
Listening to a Lecture • Listening to a Dream

Speaking
Telling Your Dreams

Connecting to the Topic

1. Why do people dream?

2. How many hours do you usually sleep? Do you feel you get enough sleep?

3. What can people do if they have trouble falling asleep? List five things.

Sleep Deprived!

Before You Listen

1 **Previewing the Conversation** Look at the photo. Ask and answer these questions with a classmate.

1. Look at Ali in the photo. Ali is "sleep deprived." What do you think this means?

2. Why do you think Ali is sleep deprived?

3. What do you think Beth and Alicia are saying to Ali?

4. Do you think Ali studies enough? Why or why not?

5. Do you think Ali usually gets enough sleep? Why or why not?

2 **Vocabulary Preview** Beth and Alicia are at a café. Ali has just arrived. Listen to these words and expressions from their conversation. Check ( ) the ones that you don't know.

Nouns	Verbs	Adjectives	Adverb	Expression
▩ advice	▩ sleep in	▩ alert	▩ hardly	▩ can't keep one's eyes open
▩ chemicals	▩ take a nap	▩ complex		
▩ research study	▩ wake up	▩ deprived		

3 **Guessing the Meanings of New Words from Context** Guess the meanings of the underlined words. Write your guess on each line. Check your answers with a dictionary or with your teacher.

1. Many people worry about the <u>chemicals</u> in food. They think some chemicals might cause cancer or other diseases.

   My guess: _____

2. A baby needs to sleep a lot. Most babies <u>take a nap</u> every day.

   My guess: _____

3. It's hard to <u>wake up</u> in the morning. I have a loud alarm clock to wake me up.

   My guess: _____

4. In Norway the days are very short in the winter. People are <u>deprived</u> of sunshine. They are very happy when spring comes.

   My guess: _____

5. A simple math problem is 2 + 6 = 8. A <u>complex</u> math problem is x [y2 324y <?> (x 2y)].

   My guess: _____

6. Oh, no! I <u>hardly</u> have any money—only 20 cents!

   My guess: _____

7. There is a lot of traffic in the city. Before you cross the street, be <u>alert</u>: Look carefully to the left and to the right and listen for cars.

   My guess: _____

8. I read a <u>research study</u> that says most Americans get only six hours of sleep a night. It was an interesting report.

   My guess: _____

9. My teacher suggested that I sleep more and go to parties less. I took her <u>advice</u>, and now I feel better!

   My guess: _____

10. I get up early every weekday, so I love to <u>sleep in</u> on the weekends.

My guess: _____

11. Ali needs to study more, but he <u>can't keep his eyes open</u>, so he's going to get some sleep.

My guess: _____

Listen

4 **Listening for Main Ideas (Part 1)** Listen to the first part of the conversation. Choose the best answer to each question.

1. What's wrong with Ali?

A He didn't get enough sleep last night.

B He went to a party last night and missed a big test today.

C both a and b

2. Who is worried about Ali and why?

A Beth is worried because Ali went to a party and didn't study last night.

B Alicia is worried because Ali only got four hours of sleep last night.

C Beth and Alicia are worried because Ali is not sleeping enough.

3. What does Alicia say about remembering what you study?

A It's important to sleep after you study.

B You should study in the morning.

C You should study late at night, after a party.

5 **Listening for Main Ideas (Part 2)** Now listen to the whole conversation. Choose the best answer to each question.

1. You may forget how much (what percent) of what you studied if you don't get enough sleep after you study?

A 30 percent

B 13 percent

C 70 percent

2. People who are sleep deprived _____.

A don't get enough sleep

B forget a lot

C both a and b

3. Beth says that eating foods like fish can help you _____.

A get enough sleep

B forget almost one-third of what you study

C study and stay alert

6 Listening for Specific Information Listen to the conversation again. Choose the best answer to each question.

1. Where did Alicia learn about sleep deprivation?
   - (A) She read a research study.
   - (B) A professor lectured about it.
   - (C) Beth told her about it.

2. If you want to remember what you study, what should you do?
   - (A) get enough sleep
   - (B) eat more food
   - (C) both a and b

3. Why do some foods help you study?
   - (A) They have chemicals that help you stay healthy.
   - (B) They have chemicals that help you stay alert.
   - (C) They have chemicals that make you sleep deprived.

After You Listen

7 Vocabulary Review Complete the sentences below. Use the words from the box.

advice	deprived	to take a nap
alert	hardly	wake me up
chemical	research	

1. My grandfather gets sleepy every afternoon, so he likes _____ for about an hour.

2. I have a test early tomorrow. Please _____ in time for class.

3. Caffeine is the _____ in coffee that keeps you awake.

4. Away from home, I felt _____ of my family and their love.

5. Drivers should always be _____. Careless or sleepy driving causes accidents.

6. Sorry! I can't go to the movies with you; I have no time and _____ any money.

7. I read an interesting _____ study that said 33 percent of the American population has sleeping problems.

8. Can you give me some _____? I need to know how to buy a used car.

Stress

8 **Listening for Stressed Words** Listen to the first part of the conversation again. Some of the stressed words are missing. Fill in the blanks with words from the box. You will use some words more than once.

before	four	in	look	party	test
big	friend	it's	lot	sleep	up
can't	going	late	matter	sleepy	
eyes	hardly	library	morning	study	

Beth: Ali! What's the _____ ? You _____
                                                   1   2

      so _____ !
                    3

Alicia: Yeah! Can't you wake _____ this morning?
                                      4

Ali: No, I _____ ! I can _____ keep my
                    5   6

    _____ open! I was up _____ last night.
            7   8

    My _____ had a _____ . I only got about
            9   10

    _____ hours of _____ .
        11   12

Alicia: Why didn't you sleep _____ this _____ ?
                            13   14

Ali: I have to meet my _____ group at the
                        15

    _____ . We have a _____
        16   17

    _____ next week.
        18

Beth: A _____ _____ ? Why didn't you
            19   20

    _____ last night instead of _____ to
        21   22

    the _____ ?
        23

Ali: Oh, _____ OK. I studied a _____
            24   25

    _____ the _____ .
        26   27

Now read the conversation in a group of three. Practice stressing words.

Pronunciation

Numbers

Numbers can be difficult to understand in spoken English. Different numbers in English sound very much the same. The difference between the "teens" (13, 14, 15) and the "tens" (30, 40, 50) is mostly stress: the ending *-teen* is stressed more than the ending *-ty*.

13 thir-téen	30 thír-ty	16 six-téen	60 síx-ty
14 four-téen	40 fór-ty	17 seven-téen	70 séven-ty
15 fif-téen	50 fíf-ty	18 eigh-téen	80 éigh-ty

9 **Pronouncing Teens and Tens** Listen and repeat these examples of teens and tens.

Teens	Tens
1. He is <u>fourteen</u> years old.	He is <u>forty</u> years old.
2. I bought <u>thirteen</u> new books.	I bought <u>thirty</u> new books.
3. The price is <u>seventeen</u> dollars.	The price is <u>seventy</u> dollars.
4. It happened in <u>1918</u>.	It happened in <u>1980</u>.
5. We stayed for <u>fifteen</u> days.	We stayed for <u>fifty</u> days.
6. I live at <u>16</u> New Hope Road.	I live at <u>60</u> New Hope Road.

10 **Distinguishing Between Teens and Tens** Listen to the sentences. Circle the letter of the sentence that you hear.

1. **a.** He is <u>fourteen</u> years old.	**b.** He is <u>forty</u> years old.
2. **a.** I bought <u>thirteen</u> new books.	**b.** I bought <u>thirty</u> new books.
3. **a.** The price is <u>seventeen</u> dollars.	**b.** The price is <u>seventy</u> dollars.
4. **a.** It happened in <u>1918</u>.	**b.** It happened in <u>1980</u>.
5. **a.** We stayed for <u>fifteen</u> days.	**b.** We stayed for <u>fifty</u> days.
6. **a.** I live at <u>16</u> New Hope Road.	**b.** I live at <u>60</u> New Hope Road.

Using the Internet

Online Dictionaries

You can use the Internet to find out the meanings of new words. Try using the keywords *online dictionary*. Combine these keywords with the keyword *English* to limit your results.

Example

online dictionary English		Submit

Remember to look at the URL (Internet address). The URL can tell you if a website is useful or not. Some dictionaries show you how to pronounce a word. If not, you can look up the word in one of the pronunciation dictionaries that you found in Chapter 4.

11 **Practicing Your Search Skills** Look on the Internet for an English online dictionary. Use the dictionary to find out the meanings of the following words. These words are related to the topic of sleep and dreams.

- oversleep
- nightmare
- insomnia
- [your choice] _____

Discuss your results with the class.

1. What keyword combinations did you use?
2. Did you check the URLs before you went to the site?
3. What do these words mean?
4. What do you think is the best online dictionary on the Internet?

Talk It Over

12 **Keeping a Dream Journal** Write down your dreams for a week. Then share your dreams with your group.

13 **Interviewing Class Members About Sleep**

1. Work in groups of four. Write the names of your group members in the spaces at the top of the chart on page 119.
2. Look at the example (Stacy).
3. As a class, practice asking your teacher the questions and write his or her answers on the chart.

   Example

   You: Do you go to bed early or late?

   Your teacher: I go to bed late.

4. Then ask your group members the questions. Write their answers on the chart.

◀ I like the morning. I'm a "morning person."

▲ I like the nighttime. I'm a "night person."

Question	Name	Teacher	Name	Name	Name
	Stacy	_____	_____	_____	_____
Do you go to bed early or late?	late				
Do you get up early or late?	late				
What do you do when you can't sleep?	I read magazines.				
Are you a "morning person" or a "night person"?	I'm a night person.				
In what language do you dream?	I dream in my native language, English.				
What kind of dreams do you enjoy the most?	I enjoy dreams where I am flying.				
Do you ever have nightmares (bad dreams)?	Yes, sometimes.				
Do you believe dreams can tell the future?	Yes, I do.				
Your question:					

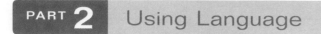

PART 2 Using Language

▲ I don't agree. I think that…

F☉CUS

Expressions for Agreeing and Disagreeing

In conversation, we show that we agree or disagree with other people. Here are some words and expressions we use to agree and disagree.

Agree	Disagree
Exactly. Of course! Great!	I don't agree… I don't know…

1 Identifying Expressions for Agreement and Disagreement Here are some more words and expressions we use to agree and to disagree. With a partner, decide which words and expressions are for agreement and which are for disagreement. Circle the words for agreement. Underline the words for disagreement.

Fabulous!	I don't think…	I'm not sure…	That's right.
Fine.	I guess so.	Perfect!	Yes, but…

2 **Listening for Main Ideas** Listen to the conversation and answer this question.

Are Lee and Alicia agreeing or disagreeing?

3 **Listening for Specific Information** Listen to the conversation again. Choose the best answer to each question.

1. How many hours a night does Alicia usually sleep?

   (A) eight   (B) nine or ten   (C) five or six

2. How many hours of sleep does Lee think is normal?

   (A) eight   (B) nine or ten   (C) five or six

3. How many hours a night does Lee usually sleep?

   (A) eight   (B) nine or ten   (C) five or six

After You Listen

4 **Expressing Disagreement** Talk with a partner. Decide if the phrases in the box below are polite or impolite. Write them in the appropriate column in the chart below. Some phrases fit in both columns.

Don't argue with me!   In my opinion…   That's a good point, but…
I don't think so.   I think it's true that…   That's wrong!
I'm not sure.   Let's not argue!   You can't say that.
I'm right.   Maybe that's right, but…   You're crazy!

Polite	Impolite

5 **Agreeing and Disagreeing** Work with a partner. Take turns. Say one of the sentences below. Your partner will agree or disagree with you, using expressions from pages 120 and 121.

1. Everyone needs the same amount of sleep.
2. It's good to go to sleep early and wake up early.
3. It's okay to sleep a little (two to four hours) on some nights and to sleep more (more than six hours) on other nights.
4. Adults need more sleep than children.
5. It's easy to sleep when the weather is cold.
6. When you exercise, you don't need much sleep.
7. It should be quiet and dark when you sleep.
8. Taking a nap in the afternoon every day is a good idea.
9. Men need to sleep more than women.
10. People should sleep more.

6 **Disagreeing with a Friend** Work with a partner. Look at the conversation below. Fill in the blanks with expressions of disagreement. There are many possible answers. Your teacher may ask you to perform your conversation for the class. The class will decide if you are disagreeing politely or impolitely!

Student A: Let's stay up all night tonight and study for the test.

Student B: _____ That's not a good idea.

Student A: _____ it is. The test is going to be really hard.

Student B: _____ if we are too tired, we won't do well on the test.

Student A: _____ If I don't study all night, I will fail the test.

Student B: _____ We can study for a few hours, then sleep.

Student A: _____

7 **Role-Play** Choose one of the situations in the boxes below and on page 123. Work with a partner. Plan a conversation between the two people in the situation. Decide if you will disagree politely or rudely. Your teacher may ask you to perform your conversation for the class.

Two friends are discussing where to go Saturday night. Person A wants to eat dinner, then go to the movies. Person B wants to go to the movies first, then eat dinner.

A student is discussing something with a parent (the student's mother or father). The student wants to pay a tutor to help him or her learn English faster. The parent wants the student to spend more time on other school subjects.

Two co-workers are discussing a problem at work. They need a new computer to help them do their work. One co-worker wants to complain to their supervisor. The other co-worker thinks the supervisor will be angry.

Getting Meaning from Context

1 **Using Context Clues** You will hear a lecture about sleep in five parts. Listen to each part and choose the best answer. Continue to listen to check each answer.

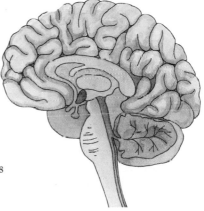

1. What are you listening to?
   - (A) a conversation
   - (B) a telephone call
   - (C) a lecture in a classroom

2. What does sleep do for your brain?
   - (A) It doesn't do anything.
   - (B) It keeps your brain healthy.
   - (C) It makes you forget things.

3. Why did Carlyle Smith teach the students a list of words and a difficult problem?
   - (A) to see if they could do the problem
   - (B) to teach them English
   - (C) to test how much they remember

4. Why did Smith have the students sleep different amounts on the first, second, and third nights?
   - (A) to see if sleeping after learning helps memory
   - (B) to see if the students became angry
   - (C) to make the students sick

5. How did the students who didn't sleep much on the first or third nights remember the difficult problem?
   - (A) They remembered the same as the other students.
   - (B) They remembered better than the students who got enough sleep.
   - (C) They didn't remember the difficult problem well.

Before You Listen

2 **Preparing to Listen** Before you listen, discuss these questions with a partner.

1. When you listen to a lecture, do you take notes? What information do you try to write down?

2. Do you review your notes before taking a test?

3. Do you try to sleep well before a test or do you stay up late studying?

Strategy

Using a Flow Chart

A graphic organizer called a *flow chart* can help you organize the steps in a process. Each step is a section of the flow chart. You will practice making a flow chart in Activity 3.

3 **Thinking About Taking Notes and Passing Tests** Fill in the flow chart below. What should a student do to get good grades? Start with "Arrive to the lecture on time (or 5 minutes early)" and end with "Take the test." When you finish, compare your chart with the rest of the class.

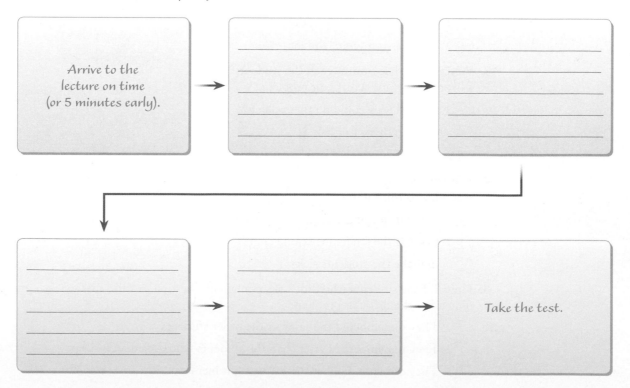

4 Vocabulary Preview Listen to these words and expressions. Check (✓) the ones that you don't know.

Nouns	Verb	Adjectives
▨ percent	▨ solve	▨ complex
▨ subject group		▨ sleep-deprived

Listen

5 Listening for Main Ideas You are going to listen to some results from the research study on sleeping. Listen and mark these statements as *T* for True or *F* for False.

1. _____ The subjects in this research study were all students.

2. _____ Being sleep-deprived affected all the subjects the same way.

3. _____ The subject groups all had the same test scores.

6 Listening for Details Listen again. Fill in the chart with the information that you hear about test scores.

Subject Group	Percent (%) Correct on the Test	
	List of Words	**Complex Problem**
Enough sleep all nights		100%
Sleep-deprived first night	100%	
Sleep-deprived second night		
Sleep-deprived third night		70%

After You Listen

7 Discussing the Lecture Work with a partner. Look at the sentences about the research study. Mark each statement as *T* for True or *F* for False. Report to the class. Does everyone agree?

1. _____ The test on the list of words showed no differences between the groups of students.

2. _____ Students who slept enough every night answered all the questions correctly.

3. _____ Students who were sleep-deprived the first night forgot the complex problem.

4. _____ Students who slept enough the first night but not the second night forgot the list of words.

5. _____ Students who slept the first night and the second night but not the third night forgot 30% of the complex problem.

6. _____ The study shows that sleeping enough is good for your memory.

Interviewing Classmates Find out how many hours each student in your class usually sleeps. Write the numbers below. Then report the results in percentages.

Example

There are 10 students in the class.

Three students usually sleep 7 hours a night.

You say: "Thirty percent of the students sleep 7 hours a night."

	Number of Students	Percentage
5 Hours		
6 Hours		
7 Hours		
8 Hours		
9 Hours		
10 Hours		

Listening to a Dream

Before You Listen

 9 Preparing to Listen Answer the questions about dreams with a partner.

1. Do you remember your dreams?
2. Do you dream in color or black and white?
3. Do you usually have pleasant dreams or unpleasant dreams?
4. Why do you think people dream when they sleep?

▼ A dream about being underwater

10 Vocabulary Preview Listen to these words and phrases. Write the words and phrases from the box under the correct picture.

bathing suit	face mask
flippers	snorkel

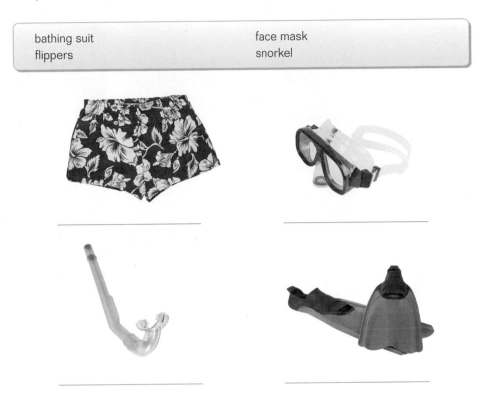

_____   _____

_____   _____

Listen

11 Listening for Main Ideas Listen to Ali talking about his dream. Circle the number of the photo that shows what happens.

▲ Photo 1

▲ Photo 2

12 Listening to a Dream Listen again. Look at the following photos. Number each photo in the order of the story.

_____

_____

_____

_____

After You Listen

13 **Discussing a Dream** Discuss these questions with a partner.

1. Where did Ali go in his dream?
2. Why couldn't Ali take off his mask and flippers?
3. How did Beth try to help Ali?
4. What happened at the end of the dream?

14 **Retelling a Dream** Now retell Ali's dream by filling in the blanks.

1. Ali dreamed that he was going _____.
2. When Ali arrived at Beth's house, he was wearing _____.
3. Beth told Ali to _____.
4. Ali couldn't do what Beth wanted because he couldn't _____

   _____.

5. Beth tried to help Ali _____.
6. Beth pulled on _____.
7. Ali fell _____ and broke _____.
8. Ali felt _____.

PART 4 Speaking

Telling Your Dreams

1 **Outlining a Dream** You are going to tell a small group about a dream you had. If you can't remember a dream, invent one. Start by making some notes about your dream on this page and page 130.

My dream about _____

The person/people in my dream: _____

_____

The first action: _____

_____

_____

The second action: _____

_____

_____

_____

The third action: _____

_____

_____

The ending: _____

_____

_____

2 **Illustrating a Dream** Draw pictures to illustrate the notes you made about your dream. Make sure you know the words to describe the objects and actions in your dream. Ask your teacher if you don't know the words you need. Write the new words on the lines below your picture.

_____

_____

3 Telling About a Dream In groups of four, tell your dream and listen to your group members' dreams. Answer these questions about the dreams you heard.

1. Who had the strangest dream?
2. Who had the scariest dream?
3. Who had the best dream?
4. Who had the most realistic dream?

Self-Assessment Log

Check (✓) the words and expressions that you learned in this chapter.

Nouns	Verbs	Adjectives	Adverb
▦ advice	▦ sleep in	▦ alert	▦ hardly
▦ chemicals	▦ solve	▦ complex	
▦ percent	▦ take a nap	▦ deprived	**Expression**
▦ research study	▦ wake up	▦ sleep-deprived	▦ can't keep one's
▦ subject group			eyes open

Check (✓) the things you did in this chapter. How well can you do each one?

	Very well	Fairly well	Not very well
I can listen for main ideas.	☐	☐	☐
I can listen for specific information.	☐	☐	☐
I can guess the meanings of words from context.	☐	☐	☐
I can identify and use stress.	☐	☐	☐
I can pronounce numbers.	☐	☐	☐
I can listen to and understand lectures.	☐	☐	☐
I can use a flow chart to organize steps in a process.	☐	☐	☐
I can use expressions for agreeing and disagreeing.	☐	☐	☐
I can use online dictionaries.	☐	☐	☐
I can talk about sleep and dreams.	☐	☐	☐

Write about what you learned and what you did in this chapter.

In this chapter,

I learned _____

_____

I liked _____

_____

7 Work and Lifestyles

"Choose a job you love, and you will never have to work a day in your life."

Confucius
Chinese philosopher

In this
CHAPTER

Using Language
Making a Complaint

Listening
Listening to Job Interviews • Listening to Future Plans

Speaking
Talking About the Future

Connecting to the Topic

1. What is happening in the photo? Describe everything you see.

2. What kind of meeting is this? What are the people discussing?

3. Is this kind of meeting good or bad? Explain why.

Looking for a Summer Job

Before You Listen

1 Prelistening Questions Ask and answer these questions with a small group.

1. Look at the photos below. Describe each job.
2. Which of these jobs would you like to have? Why?
3. What job(s) would you like to do in the future? Why?
4. Where are Alicia and Ali? What do you think they will do next?

◀ Financial analyst looking at a chart

▲ Architects discussing a project

◀ Alicia and Ali are looking for a summer job.

2 Vocabulary Preview Ali and Alicia are at the Faber College Career Planning and Placement Center. They are at the job board looking for summer jobs. Listen to these words from their conversation. Check (✓) the words that you don't know.

Nouns	Verb	Adjectives	Expression
▧ (one's) company	▧ find out	▧ full-time	▧ Don't mention it!
▧ experience		▧ part-time	
▧ journalism			
▧ public health			
▧ reporter			

3 Guessing the Meanings of New Words from Context Guess the meanings of the underlined words. Write your guesses on the lines. Check your answers with a dictionary or with your teacher.

1. Lee worked last summer for a computer software company. He got a lot of good <u>experience</u> in programming and designing computer games.

   My guess: _____

2. There are many ways to <u>find out</u> what jobs are available. You can read the paper, look on the Internet, call local companies, or ask people you know.

   My guess: _____

3. Thousands of people in my city became sick with the flu last year. This was a <u>public health</u> problem, so the government and the doctors worked together to solve the problem.

   My guess: _____

4. After the plane crash, the <u>reporter</u> had to interview the families of the passengers and then write a story about them for the newspaper.

   My guess: _____

5. Ali is still in school, so he doesn't have time for a <u>full-time</u> job. He wants a <u>part-time</u> job for about 20 hours a week.

   My guess (full-time): _____

   My guess (part-time): _____

6. Alicia is studying <u>journalism</u>. She wants to work for a newspaper or a TV news show.

   My guess: _____

7. Ali and Alicia like to do things together. They enjoy each other's <u>company</u>.

   My guess: _____

8. **Lee:** Thanks for helping me with my homework, Beth.

   Beth: <u>Don't mention it!</u>

   My guess: _____

4 **Listening for Main Ideas** Listen to the first part of the conversation. Choose the best answer to each question.

1. What are Alicia and Ali doing?

   (A) They're looking for summer jobs.

   (B) They're looking for the Placement Center.

   (C) They're looking for jobs in Maryland.

2. What kind of jobs are Ali and Alicia looking for?

   (A) jobs in their majors

   (B) jobs that they have experience in

   (C) both a and b

3. What did Ali and Alicia do last summer?

   (A) They worked full-time.

   (B) They worked part-time.

   (C) They were full-time students.

5 **Listening for Specific Information (Part 1)** Now listen to the whole conversation. Choose the best answer to each question.

1. What kind of job does Ali want?

   (A) part-time work in a lab

   (B) a job in public health

   (C) a job writing for a newspaper

2. What did Alicia do last summer?

   (A) She worked part-time for a newspaper in Mexico City.

   (B) She wrote international stories for *Excelsior*.

   (C) She traveled around Mexico.

3. How did Alicia find her job last summer?

   (A) online

   (B) in Mexico City

   (C) on a job board

6 **Listening for Specific Information (Part 2)** Listen again. Choose the best answer to each question.

1. Why did Ali come with Alicia to the Placement Center?

   (A) He wants to work for the same kind of company as Alicia.

   (B) He needs to look for a job on the Internet.

   (C) He enjoys Alicia's company, and he also needs to find a summer job.

2. Someday in the future, what does Alicia want to do?

    (A) She wants to write international news stories.

    (B) She wants to write local news stories about Mexico City for *Excelsior*.

    (C) She wants to help people around the world.

3. What does Alicia think Ali should do?

    (A) She suggests searching on the Internet.

    (B) She thinks he should look in Mexico City.

    (C) She tells him to come back to the job placement board.

After You Listen

7 **Vocabulary Review** Complete the sentences below. Use the words from the box.

company	find out	reporter
Don't mention it!	full-time	part-time
experience	journalism	public health

1. Alicia wants to get more _____ in journalism so she can get a good job after graduating.

2. A _____ might write local news stories or international news stories.

3. Students often take _____ jobs while they are in school to earn money or get experience in their majors.

4. The website for the Centers for Disease Control and Prevention at www.cdc.gov has information on _____ problems such as malaria, tuberculosis, and flu epidemics.

5. People with careers in _____ travel a lot to get information for their news stories.

6. If you want to _____ more about jobs in journalism, you should talk to someone at your local newspaper.

7. Ali, Beth, and Lee enjoy each other's _____. They spend a lot of time together.

8. A: Thank you so much for helping me with my job search!

    B: _____

9. A: Do you have a _____ job?

    B: No, I'm a student. I work part-time.

Stress

8 **Listening for Stressed Words** Listen to the first part of the conversation again. Some of the words in the box below are stressed. Fill in the blanks with words from the box.

experience	job	Maryland	reporter
great	journalism	newspaper	sure
health	looking	part-time	writing
hoping	major	public	

Alicia: What kind of _____ are you _____
1 2
for, Ali?

Ali: I'm _____ to find one in my _____
3 4
public health.

Alicia: I'm _____ you can. Do you have any
5
_____ in _____ _____?
6 7 8

Ali: Yes, I do. I worked _____ in a lab in
9
_____ last summer.
10

Alicia: That's _____. I want to find a job _____.
11 12
for a local _____. I'd like to be a _____.
13 14

Ali: Your major's _____, isn't it?
15

Now read the conversation with a partner. Practice stressing words.

Pronunciation

FOCUS

Pronouncing Majors and Job Titles

Many words for majors are similar to words for jobs. For example, someone who majors in *accounting* at a university might become an *accountant*. Notice that the last syllable tells if the word is a major or a job. The last syllable in words for majors and words for jobs is unstressed. It's important to listen carefully for the last syllable in words like these.

Examples

Major	Job Title
accoúnting	accoúntant
joúrnalism	joúrnalist

9 **Pronouncing Majors and Job Titles** Listen and repeat the following examples of majors and job titles.

Major	Job Title
accounting	accountant
psychology	psychologist
biology	biologist
journalism	journalist
physics	physicist
chemistry	chemist
economics	economist

10 **Distinguishing Between Majors and Job Titles** Listen to the sentences. Circle the letter of the major or job title that you hear.

1. **a.** journalism
   b. journalist

2. **a.** economics
   b. economist

3. **a.** psychology
   b. psychologist

4. **a.** accounting
   b. accountant

5. **a.** biology
   b. biologist

6. **a.** physics
   b. physicist

7. **a.** chemistry
   b. chemist

Using the Internet

Finding Job Information Online

You can use the Internet to get information about jobs. You can find out what certain jobs are like, how to prepare for these jobs, and their salaries. For example, if you want to know more about journalism, you can try the following keywords: *journalist job description*. To find out about how to prepare for a job, try the keywords: *journalist job preparation*, or *journalist job training*. To find organizations that hire journalists, try *journalist job openings*. To find out about salaries, type *journalist salary.*

11 **Practicing Your Search Skills** Choose a job title. Then look for a description of the job on the Internet. Also find training for the job and openings for the job. Discuss your results with the class.

1. What keyword combinations did you use?

2. Did you check the URLs before you went to the site?

3. What was the best site for your search?

4. What new things did you learn about the job?

5. What is the salary range for this job?

Talk It Over

12 Working with People, Working Alone In small groups, discuss your answers to these questions:

1. What's the best job for you?
2. Do you prefer working with people or working alone?

Strategy

Using Graphic Organizers: Cluster Charts
You can use a cluster chart to organize groups of similar ideas. Put the main idea in the center of the cluster chart. Group related ideas around the main idea. You will work with a cluster chart in Activity 13.

13 Filling in Cluster Charts Look at the cluster chart below. From the list of jobs in the box, find the jobs that involve working with people and write those jobs in the circles around the "Working with People" circle. A few examples have been done for you. Then write the jobs that involve working alone around the "Working Alone" circle. Add more lines and circles if you need to. Check with a partner to see if you agree. (Some jobs might involve both people and things.)

art/design	engineering	health care	physics
business	entertainment	hospitality/tourism	science
computers	graphic designer	manager	teacher
education			

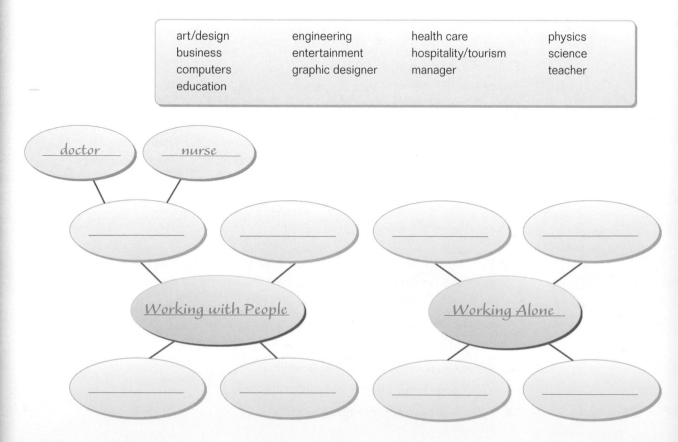

14 What Job is Best for You? Find out what job is best for you. Work with a partner. First, ask your partner the questions below. Write your partner's answers (*Yes* or *No*) in the spaces.

1. _____ Do you enjoy sitting at a computer for a long time, working or playing games?

2. _____ Do you like to work with other people to complete a task or to plan a project?

3. _____ Do you enjoy writing reports for school or work?

4. _____ Are you good at working with details, such as numbers?

5. _____ Do you like to solve problems by finding new ways of looking at them?

6. _____ Do you like to plan your own schedule and decide when you are going to work?

7. _____ Do you enjoy using your hands to build something?

8. _____ Do you like discussing problems with others to make a decision?

9. _____ Do you want a profession where you can help other people?

10. _____ Do you like to be in charge—to tell other people what to do?

11. _____ Do you work best by yourself?

12. _____ Are you happy doing the same things every day so you know what to expect?

13. _____ Do you like the challenge of learning to do new things frequently?

14. _____ Do you like to meet new people?

15. _____ Do you expect to work 12 to 14 hours a day?

16. _____ Are you happy when you know exactly what's expected of you?

17. _____ Are you good at persuading people to do what you want?

18. _____ Do you want to feel secure in your job?

19. _____ Do you like to travel?

Now look at the jobs in the box below. What job do you think is the best for your partner? Why? Tell the class why you think this is the best job for your partner.

accountant	politician
actor	programmer
bank teller	psychologist
civil engineer	restaurant manager
computer graphics designer	sales representative
hotel manager	secretary
medical doctor	teacher
medical researcher	travel writer for a magazine

Making a Complaint

F⊙CUS

Making a Complaint

Sometimes people have problems at work. They may need to talk to their supervisors. They may need to make a complaint about someone they work with. These activities will show ways to complain politely and professionally.

Before You Listen

1 Vocabulary Preview You are going to hear a conversation about a problem at work. Listen to these words and expressions. Check (✓) the ones that you don't know.

Nouns	Verbs
▦ client	▦ come up with
▦ presentation	▦ discuss

▲ Can I talk to you about something?

Listen

2 Listening for Main Ideas Listen to the conversation and answer these questions.

1. Who is the supervisor, Ann or Paula?

2. Why is Ann complaining to Paula?

3 Listening for Specific Information Listen again. Choose the best answer to each question.

1. What is Ann's problem with her job?

   Ⓐ She's late, and another account manager is doing her job.

   Ⓑ She doesn't like the other account manager.

   Ⓒ One of the other account managers is always late, so Ann has to do her job.

2. How did Ann try to solve the problem?

   Ⓐ Ann talked to the other account manager about it.

   Ⓑ Ann started coming late every day.

   Ⓒ Ann quit her job.

3. What does Paula suggest?

    (A) Ann should talk to the other account manager again.

    (B) Ann should stop complaining.

    (C) Both she and Ann should talk to the other account manager.

After You Listen

Strategy

Making Complaints Politely and Professionally
When you make a complaint you should:

- be specific about the problem
- use positive statements
- try not to get angry
- try to agree on a solution to the problem

4 **Making Complaints** Discuss the following situations with a partner. Decide if you would make a complaint in each of these situations.

1. You bought a shirt at a local store. The first time the shirt was washed, two buttons came off.

2. You ordered food in a restaurant. It was cooked too much, and it was dry when you got it.

3. You ordered food in a restaurant. The waiter brought your food, but one of the dishes was not what you ordered.

4. At your job, your supervisor asks you to do something that is not part of your job.

5. Your neighbor is making a lot of noise, and you are trying to sleep.

6. You are at a movie theater. The person behind you keeps talking, and you can't hear the movie.

7. You get a low grade on a test. You think the test was unfair.

5 **Who Do You Complain To?**

1. With a partner, choose one of the situations from Activity 4. Decide who you would complain to. For example, in Situation 1, you might complain to the manager of the store. Write a conversation. One of you will make a complaint. The other will respond appropriately. Review the complaint strategies above.

2. Then perform your conversation for the class. Did each conversation meet the four goals from the strategy you learned above?

Getting Meaning from Context

1 Vocabulary Preview Listen to these words and expressions from the conversations. Check (✓) the ones that you don't know.

Noun	**Verb**	**Adjectives**
▢ appointment	▢ get out of	▢ rough
		▢ tired of

2 Using Context Clues You will hear five conversations. Listen to each conversation and choose the best answer. Continue to listen to check your answer.

1. Who is Alicia talking to?
   - (A) an English teacher
   - (B) a reporter
   - (C) the manager of a newspaper

2. What does Sang-mi want to do this summer?
   - (A) work in a hospital
   - (B) study
   - (C) go back to Korea

3. What is Dan thinking about doing this summer?
   - (A) studying
   - (B) going to Europe
   - (C) visiting his friend in San Francisco

4. What does Dan want to do in the fall?
   - (A) work
   - (B) travel
   - (C) study

5. Can Sang-mi work?
   - (A) No, she can't.
   - (B) Yes, but only in the summer.
   - (C) Yes, but she has to finish school first.

Before You Listen

3 **Preparing to Listen** Before you listen, talk about job interviews with a partner.

1. Have you ever had an interview for a job?

2. What do you think an employer wants to know about a job applicant?

4 **Vocabulary Preview** Listen to these words and expressions. Check (✓) the ones that you don't know.

Noun
- résumé

Adjectives
- accurate
- challenging
- impressive

Listen

5 **Listening for Main Ideas**
Rafael is interviewing for a job. He's talking to Claudia. Listen to the interview and answer these questions.

1. Why is Rafael interested in the job?

2. What job would Rafael like to have in ten years?

▲ A job interview

6 **Listening for Specific Information** Listen again. This time, choose the best answer to each question.

1. Why should Claudia give Rafael a job with the company?

   Ⓐ He learns quickly.

   Ⓑ He needs the money.

   Ⓒ He thinks the job sounds easy.

2. Why does Rafael need to learn things quickly?

   Ⓐ He doesn't know anything about computers.

   Ⓑ He has to go back to school if he takes the job.

   Ⓒ He'll have to learn a lot of new things if he takes the job.

3. What would Rafael like to do in ten years?

   Ⓐ be a department store clerk

   Ⓑ be a department manager

   Ⓒ be a student

After You Listen

7 **Discussing Job Interviews** Talk in small groups. How would you answer the following common job interview questions? Think about what the interviewer wants to know. Share your answers with the class. Which answers do you think would impress an interviewer?

1. What are your strengths?
2. What are your weaknesses?
3. What is your biggest accomplishment?
4. Why do you want this job?

▲ What are some of your weaknesses?

Listening to Future Plans

Before You Listen

8 **Preparing to Listen** In small groups, talk about planning for the future. Discuss your answers to the following questions.

1. What are some situations where people ask you about your plans for the future?
2. Who do you talk to about your plans for the future? Your family? Your friends? Your teachers?

9 **Vocabulary Preview** Listen to these words and expressions. Check (✓) the ones that you don't know.

Nouns
- construction
- expenses
- relatives
- youth hostels

Expression
- once in a lifetime

Listen

10 Listening for the Main Idea Dan is talking to his father about going to Europe this summer with his friend Bill. Answer this question.

What does Dan want his father to do?

▲ Dan

Dan's father ▶

11 **Listening to Future Plans** Listen again and choose the best answer to each question.

1. What did Dan do last summer?
   - (A) traveled in Europe
   - (B) worked for a construction company
   - (C) stayed in youth hostels

2. What does Dan have to pay for on his trip?
   - (A) a rental car, hotel rooms, and meals
   - (B) airfare, hostel rooms, and meals
   - (C) airfare and a car

3. How will Dan pay for the trip?
   - (A) use money from his part-time job
   - (B) borrow money from his friend Bill
   - (C) sell his car

4. What does Dan need from his father?
   - (A) money for his books and expenses
   - (B) French lessons
   - (C) a new car

5. Which of these is NOT a reason that Dan thinks the trip is a good idea?
   - (A) He can learn about the world.
   - (B) He can earn some money.
   - (C) He can practice his French.

After You Listen

 12 **Discussing the Conversation** Discuss your answers to the following questions in small groups.

1. Do you think Dan's father will let him go to Europe with his friend?
2. What are some concerns Dan's father might have about Dan's plans?
3. What are some other reasons for going to Europe?
4. Do you think traveling is good preparation for your career? Why or why not?

Talking About the Future

1 **Class Survey** Do your classmates like to plan for the future? Take a survey and find out.

1. Work in groups of four. Look at the example (Stacy).

   Example

   A: What job do you want to have ten years from now?

   B: I want to be a software engineer.

2. As a class, practice asking your teacher the questions and write his or her answers on the chart.

3. Take turns asking your group members the questions. Write their answers on the chart.

Question	Name	Teacher	Name	Name	Name
	Stacy	_____	_____	_____	_____
What job do you want to have ten years from now?	Software engineer				
Where do you want to live ten years from now?	New York City				
What are your educational plans?	Degree in computer science				
What do you want to change about your life in the next ten years?	Wants to have a family and move to New York City				

2 **Discussing the Survey** Discuss the results of Activity 1 with the class. Make notes about the questions below.

1. What jobs do people in the class want to have?
2. Where do they want to live?
3. What do they want to change?
4. What are their plans for education?

3 **Graphing the Results** Work with your group again. Make a chart or graph showing information from the chart on page 149. Choose from the topics in the box below or write a topic of your own.

> What educational plans people have
> What field people want to work in
> Which part of the world people want to live in

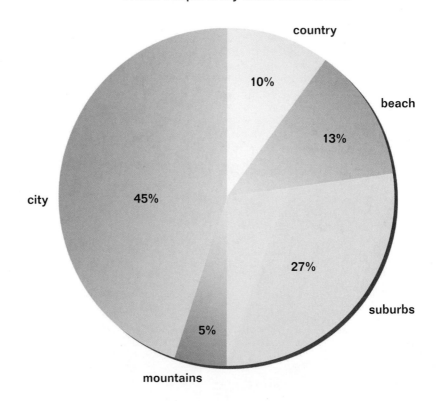

Where People in My Class Want to Live

country 10%
beach 13%
suburbs 27%
mountains 5%
city 45%

Self-Assessment Log

Check (✓) the words and expressions that you learned in this chapter.

Nouns
- appointment
- client
- (one's) company
- construction
- expenses
- experience
- journalism
- presentation
- public health
- relatives
- reporter
- résumé
- youth hostels

Verbs
- come up with
- discuss
- find out
- get out of

Adjectives
- accurate
- challenging
- full-time
- impressive
- part-time
- rough
- tired of

Idioms and Expressions
- Don't mention it!
- once in a lifetime

Check (✓) the things you did in this chapter. How well can you do each one?

	Very well	Fairly well	Not very well
I can listen for main ideas.	☐	☐	☐
I can listen for specific information.	☐	☐	☐
I can guess the meanings of words from context.	☐	☐	☐
I can identify and use stress and reductions.	☐	☐	☐
I can understand conversations about jobs and the workplace.	☐	☐	☐
I can use a cluster chart to organize information.	☐	☐	☐
I can make polite complaints.	☐	☐	☐
I can use the Internet to find information about jobs.	☐	☐	☐
I can create a pie chart to graph results.	☐	☐	☐

Write about what you learned and what you did in this chapter.

In this chapter,

I learned _____

_____

I liked _____

_____

8 Food and Nutrition

<table>
<tr><td rowspan="3">In this
CHAPTER</td><td>**Using Language**
Ordering in a Restaurant</td></tr>
<tr><td>**Listening**
Listening to Instructions • Following Recipes</td></tr>
<tr><td>**Speaking**
Talking About Recipes • Talking About Nutrition</td></tr>
</table>

Connecting to the Topic

1. Where are these people? What are they doing?

2. What kinds of foods do you see in the photo? Are these foods healthy?

3. What kinds of foods do you usually eat?

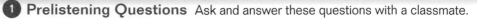

At a Food Court

Before You Listen

1 Prelistening Questions Ask and answer these questions with a classmate.

1. Look at Photo 1. Where is the woman?
2. What is the woman doing?
3. What fruits and vegetables do you usually buy?
4. How do you like to buy fruits and vegetables—fresh? Canned? Frozen? Why?
5. Look at Photo 2. Do you ever eat at food courts?
6. These days, most big shopping malls have food courts. Why do you think they are so popular?
7. How often do you eat American "fast food" such as hamburgers and French fries?
8. Do you like fast food? Why or why not?

▼ Photo 1: Shopping for produce

▲ Photo 2: Eating at a food court

2 Vocabulary Preview Dan, Meryl, and Pat are at a food court. They are deciding where to eat and what to eat. Listen to these words and expressions from their conversation. Check (✓) the ones that you don't know.

Nouns	Verbs	Adjectives	Expressions
▪ calories	▪ decide	▪ diet	▪ good/bad for you
▪ diet	▪ order	▪ worried	▪ You said it!
▪ an order of			
▪ picnic			
▪ vegetarian			

3 **Guessing the Meanings of New Words from Context**   Guess the meanings of the underlined words. Write your guesses on the lines. Check your answers with a dictionary or with your teacher.

1. Let's make some sandwiches, go to the park, and have a <u>picnic</u>.

   My guess: _____

2. Meryl eats a lot of salads, so Pat is not <u>worried</u> about Meryl's health.

   My guess: _____

3. **Waiter:**   What would you like?

   Customer: I'd like a cheeseburger and <u>an order of</u> fries.

   My guess: _____

4. He's sick because he smokes, and smoking is <u>bad for you</u>.

   My guess: _____

5. Pat doesn't eat hamburgers or other meats. She's a <u>vegetarian</u>.

   My guess: _____

6. Meryl doesn't like sugar in her food, so she will have a <u>diet</u> cola.

   My guess: _____

7. Cheeseburgers have a lot of <u>calories</u> because they have a lot of fat.

   My guess: _____

8. **Ali:**   This pizza is delicious!

   Beth: <u>You said it!</u> It is really delicious!

   My guess: _____

9. Dan loves Italian food, so he can't <u>decide</u> what to order: pizza or spaghetti.

   My guess: _____

10. **Waiter:**   What would you like to <u>order</u>?

    Customer: I'll have a double cheeseburger.

    My guess: _____

Listen

4 **Listening for Main Ideas**   Listen to the first part of the conversation. Choose the best answer to each question.

1. What are Dan, Meryl, and Pat doing?

   Ⓐ They are waiting in line at a restaurant.

   Ⓑ They are eating at a food court.

   Ⓒ They are deciding what to eat.

2. Where is Dan going to eat?

    Ⓐ at a fast-food restaurant

    Ⓑ at a picnic because he likes cheeseburgers

    Ⓒ at a vegetarian restaurant

3. What do Pat and Meryl think?

    Ⓐ Dan eats too many cheeseburgers.

    Ⓑ Cheeseburgers are good for you.

    Ⓒ both a and b

5 Listening for Specific Information (Part 1) Now listen to the whole conversation. Choose the best answer to each question.

1. Who is *not* going to order a cheeseburger and why?

    Ⓐ Pat is not going to order a cheeseburger because she's a vegetarian.

    Ⓑ Meryl is not going to order a cheeseburger because she's on a diet.

    Ⓒ both a and b

2. Who is going to have a salad?

    Ⓐ Meryl only

    Ⓑ Dan only

    Ⓒ both Meryl and Dan

3. What is bad about cola and other sodas?

    Ⓐ They have a lot of sugar.

    Ⓑ They are bad for your teeth.

    Ⓒ both a and b

6 Listening for Specific Information (Part 2) Listen to the whole conversation again. Choose the best answer to each question.

1. At the beginning of the conversation, Pat can't decide what to have. Why not?

    Ⓐ She's a vegetarian, and there are no vegetarian choices.

    Ⓑ She's on a diet, and there are no places to order a salad.

    Ⓒ There are so many choices at the food court.

2. Why are Pat and Meryl worried about Dan?

    Ⓐ He eats a lot of fast food.

    Ⓑ He's fat.

    Ⓒ He drinks a lot of soda.

3. Who orders a diet soda and why?

    Ⓐ Pat does because she's a vegetarian.

    Ⓑ Meryl does because there's no sugar in it.

    Ⓒ Dan does because he's worried about his teeth.

7 Vocabulary Review Complete these sentences. Use words from the box.

bad for you	diet	to order
calories	order of	worried
decide	picnic	You said it!

1. Foods with a lot of sugar, like soft drinks, usually have a lot of

   _____ in them.

2. Meryl and Pat are _____ about Dan's health because he eats

   too many cheeseburgers.

3. Do you think _____ foods really help you lose weight?

4. We can take a long walk and eat a _____ outside along the way.

5. Doctors think that foods with a lot of fat, such as red meat and ice cream, are

   _____.

6. With my tofu, I'd like a side _____ rice, please.

7. **Waiter:** What would you like _____?

   Customer: I can't _____. What's good on the menu tonight?

8. **Dan:** Look at all these places to eat! This food court is great!

   Pat: _____.

   It is great!

Stress

8 Listening for Stressed Words Listen to the first part of the conversation again. Some of the stressed words are missing. Fill in the blanks with words from the box. You may use some words more than once.

cheeseburger	fast	have	like	place
eat	food	healthy	order	what
fat	fries	hungry	picnic	worried

Meryl: What are you going to _____, Dan?
                                          1

Dan: I'm _____! I'm going to the _____
                      2   3

_____ _____. I want a double
          4   5

_____ and a large _____ of
          6   7

_____.
          8

Pat: Ugh! How many cheeseburgers do you _____ every
9

week? You had a couple at the _____ yesterday,
10

didn't you?

Dan: Yeah... so _____? I _____
11   12

cheeseburgers!

Meryl: I think Pat's _____ about you.
13

Dan: Why? I'm _____.
14

Pat: But cheeseburgers have a lot of _____.
15

Now read the conversation with a partner. Practice stressing words.

Reductions

❾ Comparing Long and Reduced Forms Listen to the sentences. Repeat them after the speaker. Note that the reduced forms (*) are not correct written forms of words.

Long Form	Reduced Form
1. What are you going to have?	What're* ya gonna* have?
2. I think I'm going to have some tofu and rice.	I think I'm gonna* have some tofu 'n* rice.
3. We would like a couple of salads.	We'd like a coupla* salads.
4. Isn't there a lot of fat in cheeseburgers?	Isn't there a lotta* fat in cheeseburgers?
5. They don't want to eat lots of fatty food.	They don't wanna* eat lotsa* fatty food.

❿ Listening for Reductions Listen and circle the letter of the sentence that you hear. Note that the reduced forms (*) are not the correct written forms of words.

1. **a.** What are you going to have?

   b. What're* ya* gonna* have?

2. **a.** I think I am going to have some tofu and rice.

   b. I think I'm gonna* have some tofu 'n* rice.

3. **a.** We would like a couple of salads.

   b. We'd like a coupla* salads.

4. **a.** Isn't there a lot of fat in cheeseburgers?

   b. Isn't there a lotta* fat in cheeseburgers?

5. **a.** They don't want to eat lots of fatty food.

   b. They don't wanna* eat lotsa* fatty food.

Using the Internet

Finding Information About Food

You can find information about food and diets on the Internet. Combine keywords to find out things like the fat, calorie, and sugar content in foods. You can also find calorie counters on the Internet. A calorie counter will tell you how many calories are in a particular food.

Examples

| calories   apple | Submit |

| calorie counter | Submit |

You can also go to sites that have information about food and diets.
Some of these are the United States Department of Agriculture (USDA) at
www.choosemyplate.gov, the World Health Organization (WHO) at www.who.int/en,
or the British Broadcasting Corporation (BBC) at www.bbc.co.uk/health.

11 Practicing Your Search Skills Look on the Internet for information about food and diets. Find the following:

- a caloric counter
- how many calories a medium-sized apple has
- how many calories your favorite snack food has
- how many calories your favorite drink has
- what you can learn from one of the food information sites above (the WHO, the BBC, or the USDA)
- how many calories you should eat each day
- [your own idea]

Discuss your results with the class.

1. What keyword combinations did you use?
2. Did you check the type of URLs before you went to the site?
3. What was the best site for your searches?
4. What new things did you learn about food and diets?

Strategy

Categorizing Vocabulary Words

When you learn a new vocabulary word, it can be helpful to put that new word into a category. For example, the word *apple* goes in the category *fruit*. It can also be helpful to put words into groups. This will help you remember words and learn new words. You will practice categorizing words in Activity 12 and in another activity later in the chapter.

12 Discussing Healthy and Unhealthy Foods With a partner, talk about the food items in the box below. Is each item good for you or bad for you? Write each item in the appropriate column in the chart on page 161. Then add the reason each item is good for you or bad for you. Discuss your decisions with the class.

Fast food is bad for you. ▶

▲ Fresh produce is good for you.

beans	fruit	salad dressing
bread	ice cream	skim (nonfat) milk
cheeseburgers	meat	soda
eggs	orange juice	tofu
French fries	rice	vegetables

Good for You	Bad for You	Reason
	French fries	They have a lot of fat.

Ordering in a Restaurant

Before You Listen

1 Vocabulary Preview You are going to hear Lee and Alicia order dinner in a restaurant. Listen to these words and expressions. Check (✓) the ones that you don't know.

Nouns
- check
- dessert
- dressing
- hot tea
- menu
- mushroom

Verb
- order

Listen

2 Listening for the Main Idea Lee and Alicia are doing something special tonight. Listen to the conversations and answer the question.

Are Lee and Alicia having dinner with a group of friends?

3 **Listening for Specific Information** Look at the photos and listen to the conversations again. Number each photo to match the number of the conversation that you hear.

_____

_____

_____

_____

_____

4 **Ordering in a Restaurant** Now listen to the conversations again. Write the sentences that Lee and Alicia use to ask for each of the following items.

1. a table near the window _____

2. water _____

3. the mushroom tortellini _____

4. the spaghetti with tomato sauce _____

5. some lemon for the tea _____

6. the check _____

After You Listen

5 **Role-Play** Work in groups of three. Two students are customers, and one student is the waiter. The customers order from the menu below. Use the words and expressions from the box. Then, perform your role-play for the class.

Menu Words

| an appetizer | salad dressing | soup | salad |
| drink | entrée | dessert | |

Customer Expressions

| I'd like… | Could I have… | I'll have… | Would you bring us… |

Waiter/Waitress Expressions

| Would you like… | What kind of… | What would you like… |

Mary's RESTAURANT

APPETIZERS

Oysters on the Half Shell – dozen $8.95, half dozen $5.95
Stuffed Artichoke $4.95
Nachos $4.95   Nachos with Guacamole $5.95

SOUPS

Soup of the Day $2.95   French Onion Soup $2.50

SALADS

Spinach Salad $3.75   Small Tossed Salad $2.95
Dressings: French, Italian, Ranch

ENTREES

Hamburger $5.95 – with Cheese $6.50
Chile con Carne $7.25   Grilled Chicken $8.95
Stuffed Green Peppers $9.50   Sesame Tofu $8.50
Pesto Pasta $9.50
Entrees come with baked potato or rice and vegetables.

DESSERTS

Cheesecake $3.50   Chocolate Cake $3.95
Pecan Pie $2.95   Ice Cream $2.50

BEVERAGES

Coffee $1.25   Tea $1.25   Soft Drinks $1.25

We take Visa, MasterCard, and American Express. • 5% tax added to all items

Thank you for eating at Mary's

Getting Meaning from Context

1 Vocabulary Preview You are going to hear some conversations about food. Listen to these words and expressions from the conversations. Check (✓) the ones that you don't know.

Nouns
- carrot
- charge
- cucumber
- onion soup
- ounce
- produce
- teaspoon

Verb
- beat

2 Using Context Clues You will hear five conversations. Listen to each conversation and choose the best answer. Continue to listen to check each answer.

1. Where are Lee and Alicia?
   - (A) in a restaurant
   - (B) in a supermarket
   - (C) in a cafeteria

2. What's Lee asking about?
   - (A) the waiter
   - (B) the menu
   - (C) the bill

3. What are Dan and Beth doing?
   - (A) cooking something
   - (B) shopping
   - (C) eating in a restaurant

4. Where are Ali and Alicia?
   - (A) at a restaurant
   - (B) at a produce stand (a small fruit and vegetable market)
   - (C) in a supermarket produce (fruit and vegetable) section

5. Which spaghetti sauce is the best price?
   - (A) the smaller can
   - (B) the eight-ounce size for $1.06
   - (C) the sauce for $0.99

Before You Listen

3 Preparing to Listen Work with a partner to answer the questions.

1. When do you give someone instructions? List some possible situations. Share with the class.

2. Do you cook? What do you know how to cook?

3. What food would you like to learn how to cook? Why?

4 Vocabulary Preview Listen to these words and expressions from the conversation. Check (✓) the ones that you don't know.

Noun	Verbs	Adverb
▢ cheese grater	▢ brown	▢ thoroughly
	▢ chop	
	▢ grate	

Listen

5 Listening for Main Ideas Beth and Alicia are talking to Ali. Listen to their conversation and answer these questions.

1. What kind of instructions did Ali's mother send him?

2. Why did Ali ask his mother for recipes?

6 Listening to Instructions Listen again. This time, match the words on the left with the meanings on the right. Then, listen again to check your answers. Compare your answers with a partner.

1. ____ ____ chop   **a.** a tool for making small, thin pieces of cheese

2. ____ mix   **b.** cook something in oil until it changes color

3. ____ grate   **c.** cut something into small pieces

4. ____ brown   **d.** combine two or more things together

5. ____ cheese grater   **e.** make thin, little pieces of cheese or other foods

◀ cheese grater

◀ grated (or shredded) cheese

After You Listen

7 **Categorizing Food** If you want to learn new recipes, you need to know the names of many different food items. How many do you know in English?

1. Work in groups of four. Each member of the group chooses one letter of the alphabet. Write one letter in each of the four boxes across the top of the following chart.

2. Write a word in each space that fits the category and starts with the letter at the top of the column. Do the first column as a class. For example, the letter for column 1 is S. For the category *Fruits*, you can write "Strawberry." Fill in as many spaces as you can in three minutes with your class.

3. Now, complete the activity with your small group. When you finish, take turns reading your answers in your group. Cross off any answers that another member in the group says. You get one point for each answer you wrote that no one else has. The person with the most points wins.

Category	S				
Fruits	Strawberry				
Vegetables					
Grains					
Meats					
Desserts					
Drinks					

Before You Listen

8 **Preparing to Listen** Before you listen, talk about cooking and recipes with a partner.

1. What is a recipe you know? Describe it.
2. What is a cooking show? Describe them. Do you watch cooking shows?

9 **Vocabulary Preview** Match the food words below with the photos. Write the letter of the photo on the correct line.

a.

b.

c.

d.

e.

f.

g.

1. _____ beef
2. _____ beans
3. _____ tomatoes
4. _____ onion

5. _____ oil
6. _____ chili powder
7. _____ shredded cheese

Listen

10 **Listening for the Main Idea** Wally Chan has a cooking show on TV. He explains how to make easy American dishes. As you listen to Wally Chan's show, answer this question.

What food is Wally making?

◀ Wally Chan chopping onions

11 **Ordering Steps in a Recipe** Look at these photos. They show the steps for making chili, but the steps are in the wrong order. Listen to Wally's show again and number the photos from 1 to 4.

_____   _____

_____   _____

After You Listen

12 **Discussing Opinions About Food** Listen to the following statements. Decide if you agree or disagree. Write *A* for Agree or *D* for Disagree for each of the statements. Then, compare your answers with the class.

1. _____ I like onions on my hamburgers.

2. _____ Chili powder makes food too hot and spicy.

3. _____ I eat a lot of cheese—with crackers, bread, and other foods.

4. _____ Tomatoes are best in salad, with lettuce, oil, and vinegar.

5. _____ I like beans when they are cooked with onions and garlic.

6. _____ Cooking with oil can make you fat.

7. _____ The best pizza has just tomato sauce and lots of cheese.

8. _____ Foods like beans, rice, and potatoes should be eaten at every meal.

9. _____ Onions are good cooked and uncooked.

10. _____ I like a lot of salt in my food.

PART 4 Speaking

Talking About Recipes

1 **Discussing Recipes**

1. Work in groups of three. Each person chooses a different recipe card (Recipe A, Recipe B, or Recipe C from pages 170–171). Do not look at the recipe cards of the other two people in your group.

2. First, ask and answer questions to get the missing ingredients.

   Example

   Student A: What ingredients do you have?

   Student B: I have 2 tablespoons chopped onion.

   Student C: I have 1 pound ground beef. What ingredients do you have?

   Student A: I have 6 large green peppers.

3. Then, ask and answer questions to get the missing steps for making stuffed green peppers.

4. When you have all the steps, put them in the correct order. Mark the order of the steps on the recipe card in the Steps column.

Recipe for Stuffed Peppers

Ingredients

6 large green peppers   3/4 cup shredded cheese

Steps	Steps
• Stuff each pepper with ground beef mixture.	
• Cook peppers in boiling water for 5 minutes.	3
• Sprinkle with shredded cheese.	

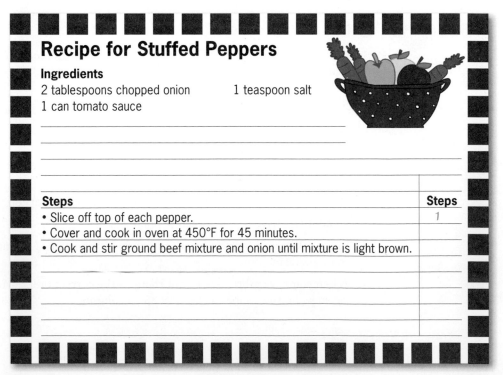

Student B

Recipe for Stuffed Peppers

Ingredients

2 tablespoons chopped onion   1 teaspoon salt
1 can tomato sauce

Steps	Steps
• Slice off top of each pepper.	1
• Cover and cook in oven at 450°F for 45 minutes.	
• Cook and stir ground beef mixture and onion until mixture is light brown.	

Recipe for Stuffed Peppers

Ingredients

1 pound ground beef   1 cup cooked rice
1/8 teaspoon garlic salt

_____

_____

_____

Steps	Steps
• Remove seeds from peppers.	2
• Stir in garlic, salt, rice, and one cup of the tomato sauce.	
• Pour remaining tomato sauce over peppers.	

2 **Writing a Recipe** Think about a dish that you can cook. Write some notes about how to cook it and list the ingredients. Then write the steps to prepare it.

Ingredients	Steps
_____	What do you do first? _____
_____	_____
_____	_____
_____	Next? _____
_____	_____
_____	Next? _____
_____	_____
_____	Next? _____
_____	_____

In groups of four, take turns presenting your dish. Tell the other students how to prepare it.

Talking About Nutrition

3 Discussing Contents of Food Talk in a group of four or five. Which of the following do you think about when you decide what to eat?

calories	cholesterol	protein	sugar
carbohydrates	fat	salt	vitamins

4 Comparing Food Labels Bring in a label from some food that you eat—a box, bag, or can. In groups, compare your labels. Which food has the most/least of the following ingredients? Complete the chart as you talk.

calories	fat	protein	sodium	sugar	vitamins

Food	Has the Most...	Has the Least...
potato chips	sodium	vitamins

Self-Assessment Log

Check (✓) the words and expressions that you learned in this chapter.

Nouns
- an order of
- calories
- carrot
- charge
- check
- cheese grater
- cucumber
- dessert
- diet
- dressing
- hot tea
- menu
- mushroom
- onion soup
- ounce
- picnic
- produce
- teaspoon
- vegetarian

Verbs
- beat
- brown
- chop
- decide
- grate
- order

Adjectives
- diet
- good/bad for you
- worried about

Adverb
- thoroughly

Expression
- You said it!

Check (✓) the things you did in this chapter. How well can you do each one?

	Very well	Fairly well	Not very well
I can listen for main ideas.	☐	☐	☐
I can listen for specific information.	☐	☐	☐
I can guess the meanings of words from context.	☐	☐	☐
I can identify and use stress and reductions.	☐	☐	☐
I can understand instructions and recipes.	☐	☐	☐
I can categorize vocabulary words.	☐	☐	☐
I can use my Internet search skills to find information about food.	☐	☐	☐
I can talk about recipes and nutrition.	☐	☐	☐
I can put steps of a recipe in order.	☐	☐	☐
I can order in a restaurant.	☐	☐	☐
I can talk about food and nutrition.	☐	☐	☐

Write about what you learned and what you did in this chapter.

In this chapter,

I learned _____

_____

I liked _____

_____

9 Great Destinations

"No man should travel
until he has learned
the language of the
country he visits."

Ralph Waldo Emerson
U.S. author, poet,
and philosopher

In this
CHAPTER

Using Language
Persuading Others

Listening
Listening to a Tour Guide • Listening for Flight Information

Speaking
Planning a Trip

Connecting to the Topic

1. Who are these people? What are they doing?

2. What kinds of activities do you think they are doing on their trip?

3. Where have you traveled to? What kinds of activities have you done in your travels?

Arriving in San Francisco

1 **Prelistening Questions** Look at the photos and answer the questions with a classmate.

1. Look at Photo 1. What city is this? How do you know?

2. Look at Photo 2. What city is this? What do you know about this city? Where is this city? How's the weather there? What is it like in the winter? What is it like in the summer? What are some things you can see and do there?

3. Do you like to visit big cities? Why or why not?

4. What interesting places in your country have you visited or do you know about?

5. What place around the world would you most like to visit? Why?

6. Do you prefer to fly, drive, or take the train when you travel? Why?

▲ Photo 2

2 **Vocabulary Preview** It is spring break. Dan, Beth, and Ali are driving to San Francisco. They are just now arriving in the city. Listen to these words and expressions from their conversation. Check () the ones that you don't know.

Nouns		Verbs	Adjective
▢ criminal	▢ skyline	▢ change (a tire)	▢ triangular
▢ flat tire	▢ spare tire	▢ explore	
▢ landmark	▢ tower	▢ pull over	**Expression**
▢ prison			▢ can't wait

▼ Photo 1

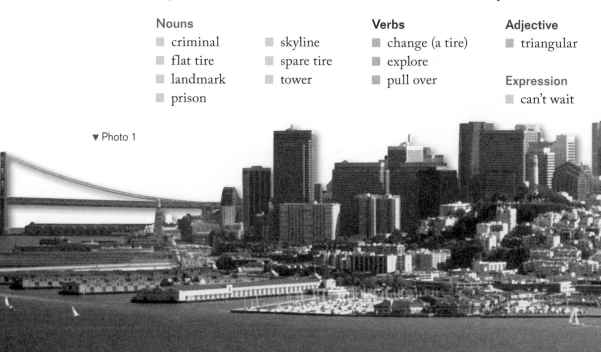

3 Guessing the Meanings of New Words from Context Guess the meanings of the underlined words. Write your guesses on the lines. Check your answers with a dictionary or with your teacher.

1. New York's <u>skyline</u> is world famous. You can see many tall buildings and the Statue of Liberty.

   My guess: _____

2. A car has five tires: one on each wheel and one called a <u>spare tire</u>.

   My guess: _____

3. My car has a <u>flat tire</u>. I think there's a hole in it.

   My guess: _____

4. I'm going to <u>pull over</u> to the side of the road and stop the car.

   My guess: _____

5. I had to <u>change</u> the flat tire. Now I need to buy a new tire to replace the spare tire.

   My guess: _____

6. The pyramids in Egypt have <u>triangular</u> sides.

   My guess: _____

7. Bonnie and Clyde were famous American <u>criminals</u> who lived in the 1920s. They robbed a lot of banks and killed several people.

   My guess: _____

8. After the man robbed a bank, he was put in <u>prison</u> for six years.

   My guess: _____

9. My family and I are going to Disneyland next month. My kids <u>can't wait</u> to meet Mickey Mouse!

   My guess: _____

10. London's Big Ben and the Eiffel Tower in Paris are famous <u>landmarks</u>.

    My guess: _____

11. **Ali:**   What's that tall building over there?

    Beth: It's not a building. It's a water <u>tower</u>. It holds fresh water.

    My guess: _____

12. I love to <u>explore</u> interesting cities for the first time. I look for good restaurants, new stores for shopping, and places with good nightlife.

    My guess: _____

4 **Listening for Main Ideas (Part 1)** Listen to the first part of the conversation. Choose the best answer to each question.

1. What are Dan, Beth, and Ali enjoying?
   - Ⓐ visiting San Francisco
   - Ⓑ looking at the San Francisco skyline
   - Ⓒ the tour of Alcatraz

2. What is the Transamerica Building?
   - Ⓐ a San Francisco landmark and part of the San Francisco skyline
   - Ⓑ a triangular tower
   - Ⓒ both a and b

3. What is Alcatraz?
   - Ⓐ a prison where dangerous criminals are put
   - Ⓑ a former prison and an interesting place to tour
   - Ⓒ a famous bridge

5 **Listening for Main Ideas (Part 2)** Now listen to the whole conversation. Choose the best answer to each question.

1. What does Dan say he wants to do tomorrow?
   - Ⓐ visit Alcatraz
   - Ⓑ see all of San Francisco's famous landmarks
   - Ⓒ change the flat tire

2. Why does Dan pull the car over?
   - Ⓐ because the car has a flat tire
   - Ⓑ because they (Dan, Beth, and Ali) need to get to San Francisco
   - Ⓒ because they want to visit Alcatraz

3. What does Ali say about the flat tire?
   - Ⓐ It will take a long time to change it.
   - Ⓑ It will take a short time to change it.
   - Ⓒ Dan and Beth can change it.

▼ Ali

Beth ▶

◀ Dan

6 Listening for Specific Information Listen again. Choose the best answer to each question.

1. Ali says, "I can't wait to go to all those places." What does he mean?
   - (A) He's excited about visiting San Francisco's famous landmarks.
   - (B) He's going to visit San Francisco's famous landmarks today.
   - (C) He wants to visit just Alcatraz.

2. What does Dan want to do tomorrow?
   - (A) visit Alcatraz all day
   - (B) visit Alcatraz, perhaps in the morning or the afternoon
   - (C) visit all of San Francisco's landmarks

3. How long will it take to change the flat tire?
   - (A) a few minutes
   - (B) all afternoon
   - (C) a day

After You Listen

Strategy

Using a Graphic Organizer: T-charts

To compare two things, you can make a graphic organizer called a T-chart. For example, you can compare two places by using a T-chart. Label one column with one place and the other column with the other place. Write words describing each place below the labels. Group the negative words and the positive words. A T-chart can help you choose which place is better. The T-chart below compares two places: the beach and the mountains. You will practice making a T-chart to compare two places in Activity 7.

The Beach	The Mountains
warm	cold
sand	snow
water	ice
vacation place	vacation place
swimming	skiing
bathing suit	coat

7 **Using a T-chart to Compare Two Places** Work with a partner. Decide which of the words in the box below describe San Francisco, California. Decide which of the words in the box describe the Grand Canyon. Some words may describe both places. Write the words in the appropriate column on the T-chart. Add a few words of your own.

▲ San Francisco

▲ The Grand Canyon

beautiful	dry	lively	peaceful	wild
calm	exciting	modern	rugged	
colorful	famous	natural	uncrowded	

San Francisco	Grand Canyon

Now look at the T-chart and compare San Francisco to the Grand Canyon. Answer this question with your partner.

Which place would you like to visit? Why?

With your partner, think of two places you would like to visit. Make a T-chart like the one above comparing your two places.

Stress

8 Listening for Stressed Words Listen to the first part of the conversation again. Some of the stressed words are missing. Fill in the blanks with words from the box. Some words may be used more than once.

almost	Francisco's	places	There's
Bridge	landmarks	skyline	tower
famous	Look	tall	triangular
Francisco	looks	That's	wait

Beth: _____ , guys, up ahead! _____ San

　　　　　1　　　　　　　　　　　　　　　2
_____! We're almost there!

　　　3

Ali: _____ at that _____! What's that

　　　4　　　　　　　　　　5
_____ , _____ building? It

　　　6　　　　　　　　　7
_____ like a _____.

　　　8　　　　　　　　　9

Dan: _____ the Transamerica Building. It's one of San

　　　10
_____ _____. It's _____

　　　11　　　　　　　　12　　　　　　　　　　　13
as _____ now as the Golden Gate _____ ,

　　　14　　　　　　　　　　　　　　　　　15
the cable cars, Chinatown…

Ali: Well, I can't _____ to go to all those

　　　　　　　　16
_____ … and Alcatraz, too.

　　　17

Now read the conversation in a group of three. Practice stressing words.

FOCUS

Word Families and Stress

A word family is a group of related nouns, verbs, adjectives, or adverbs. For example, *photograph, photography, photographic.* The different words in a word family have different stress.

Examples

pho'tography (n)	'photograph (n and v)	photo'graphic (adj)
edu'cation (n)	'educate (v)	edu'cational (adj)
exami'nation (n)	e'xamine (v)	
'record (n)	re'cord (v)	
bi'ography (n)		bio'graphical (adj)

9 Stress and Word Families Listen to the word families below. Repeat each word after the speaker.

1. photógraphy (n) phótograph (n and v) photográphic (adj)
2. récord (n) recórd (v)
3. désert (n) desért (v) desérted (adj)
4. bénefit (n) bénefit (v) benefícial (adj)
5. biógraphy (n)   biográphical (adj)
6. análysis (n) ánalyze (v) análytical (adj)
7. examinátion (n) exámine (v)
8. educátion (n) éducate (v) educátional (adj)

10 Listening for Stress Listen to the sentences. Mark the stress of the underlined word.

1. <u>Photography</u> is a popular hobby.
2. The <u>desert</u> is a bad place to have a flat tire.
3. I keep good <u>records</u> of my income and expenses.
4. The medicine had a <u>beneficial</u> effect on the patient.
5. I have class tonight, so please <u>record</u> my favorite TV program for me.
6. You must pass the <u>examination</u> to pass the course.
7. Schools try to <u>educate</u> every student equally.
8. I need to <u>analyze</u> the results of my research.
9. I read Ulysses Grant's <u>biography</u> for my history course.
10. Please take a <u>photograph</u> of us in front of the monument.

Using the Internet

Finding Photos on the Internet

Photographs can give you a great deal of information. They can help you understand new ideas. Photos are also useful for learning about new places and for planning travel.

Here's one way to find photos on the Internet: Go to a search engine such as Google. Click on "Images." In the text box, type keywords that describe the pictures you want.

Example

| Everything | **Images** | Maps | Videos | News |

| Grand Canyon | Submit

Use the keyword and search skills that you learned in this book.

Practicing Your Search Skills Practice looking for photos on the Internet. Look for photos of places. Try to find photos of the following. If possible, print your photos and bring them to class.

- San Francisco
- the Grand Canyon
- a famous landmark
- your favorite place to visit
- a place you would like to visit

Discuss your results with the class.

1. What keyword combinations did you use?
2. Did you check the URLs before you went to the site?
3. Who found the best photos?

Talk It Over

 Describing Photos Look at the photos below. Describe one of the photos to your group. Don't tell them which photo you are describing. Your group will guess which photo you are describing.

Example Many people visit this place every year to ski.

◄ Photo 1

▲ Photo 2

▼ Photo 4

▲ Photo 3

Persuading Others

F☉CUS

Expressions For Persuading Others

When you talk to people at work, at school, and in other places, you often want to persuade them to do something. This is called *persuasion*. The vocabulary list in Activity 1 shows some expressions you can use to persuade other people.

Before You Listen

1 **Vocabulary Preview** You are going to hear a conversation consisting of suggestions and persuasion. Listen to these words and expressions from the conversation. Check (✓) the ones that you don't know.

Noun	**Verb**	**Expressions**	
■ the way back	■ should	■ Couldn't we…	■ Sounds good/OK
		■ I'd rather…	■ Wouldn't you rather
		■ Let's	

Listen

2 **Listening for Main Ideas** Listen to the conversations. Number the photos to match Conversation 1, Conversation 2, or Conversation 3.

3 Listening for Specific Information Listen to the conversations again and fill in the chart below. Where do Ali, Beth, and Ming want to go? What reasons do they give?

Person	Place They Want to Go	Reasons They Give
Ali		
Beth		
Ming		

After You Listen

Ways Men and Women Persuade Others

Some experts say that in the United States, men usually use statements to make suggestions or to persuade. For example, in the conversations in Activity 2, Lee, Ali, and Dan made these statements:

Lee: Ali, it's a perfect day to go to the beach. **Let's go**!

Ali: I'd rather go on a bike ride. **Come and ride up** to the Prospect Park Lake with me.

Dan: There's a new Mexican restaurant on Poplar. **Let's go** there.

On the other hand, women often ask questions or use words such as *could* and *would*. For example, in the conversations in Activity 2, Alicia, Beth, and Ming say:

Alicia: Hey, Beth. **Do you want to go** shopping at the mall today?

Beth: I think I've been spending too much money lately. **Wouldn't you rather go** for a nice walk in the mountains?

Ming: Oh, I ate there last night. It was a little too spicy for me. **Couldn't we go** to Wang's instead?

4 How Do You Persuade Others? In small groups, discuss the following questions. Report your discussion to the class.

1. In your native language, do you think that men and women use different ways to persuade others?

2. If you are a woman, do you usually make statements or ask questions to persuade someone? If you are a man, do you usually make statements or ask questions to persuade someone? Discuss with your group.

Expressions For Making Suggestions and Expressing Opinions

The following expressions will help you make suggestions and give your opinion.

Making Suggestions		**Expressing Opinions**
Let's go	(to the beach.)	I'd like to go (to the mountains.)
We could go	(swimming.)	I don't like to go (fishing.)
Would you like to go	(to a lake?)	I'd rather go (waterskiing.)
Wouldn't you like to go	(camping?)	
Would you rather go	(to a big city?)	
Wouldn't you rather go	(sightseeing?)	

5 Persuading Others

1. In a small group, plan a trip you want to take together. Choose a place from the photos below or choose your own idea. Persuade the people in your group to go there. Use the expressions in the box above and the words in the boxes below.

2. As a group, choose the most exciting trip.

3. When you finish, tell the class where your group is going and why.

Trip #1: To the beach

Activities:
Swimming
Sunbathing
Walking in the sand

Trip #2: To a lake in the mountains

Activities:
Fishing
Boating and waterskiing
Hiking

Trip #3: To a big city

Activities:
Sightseeing
Shopping
Dining out
Going to the museums

Trip #4: To an amusement park

Activities:
Riding the roller coaster
Playing games for prizes
Seeing shows

Trip #5: To the countryside

Activities:
Driving
Eating
Exploring
Walking

Trip #6: [Your idea]

_____

_____

Activities:

_____

_____

_____

_____

Getting Meaning from Context

1 Vocabulary Preview Dan, Beth, and Ali are on another trip. This time they are in the southwestern United States. Listen to these words and expressions from their conversation. Check (✓) the ones that you don't know.

Nouns
- advisory
- fishing equipment
- flash flood
- luggage
- sleeping bag
- tent
- trunk

Verb
- take up space

Adjective
- freezing

▲ Driving through New Mexico in the southwestern United States.

Ali ▶

Beth ▶

Dan ▶

2 Using Context Clues You will hear five conversations. Listen to each conversation and choose the best answer. Continue to listen to check each answer.

1. What did Beth, Dan, and Ali finish doing?
   - (A) changing a flat tire
   - (B) putting everything in the car
   - (C) taking everything out of the car

2. What are Beth, Dan, and Ali going to do?
   - (A) eat a picnic lunch in the desert
   - (B) look at a map
   - (C) find a restaurant

3. Why is Dan going to turn on the radio?
   - (A) to listen to some music
   - (B) to hear a weather report
   - (C) to find something to listen to

4. What's the weather probably going to be like tonight?
   - (A) rainy and hot
   - (B) cloudy and cool
   - (C) rainy and cold

5. Why is Dan sorry?
   - (A) He didn't listen to the weather report.
   - (B) He didn't want to go camping in the rain.
   - (C) He didn't see a stop sign.

Listening to a Tour Guide

Before You Listen

3 Preparing to Listen Before you listen, talk about sightseeing with a partner.

1. Do you like to go sightseeing?
2. What kinds of places do you like to visit?
3. What city in the world do you think is good for sightseeing?
4. What is your favorite sight to see in your hometown or your city?
5. What are some other sights in your hometown or your city?

4 Vocabulary Preview Match the words and expressions with the photos below. Look at the example.

1. __b__ interstate highway   4. _____ amusement park
2. _____ capitol building   5. _____ fountain
3. _____ Civil War general   6. _____ graves

a.   b.   c.

e.

d.

f.

Listen

5 Listening for Main Ideas You are going to go on a sightseeing tour of a major U.S. city. The tour guide is going to describe some interesting sights in the city. As you listen, answer these questions.

1. What state are you in? _____

2. What city are you touring? _____

6 Listening for Places on a Map Listen again. This time, look at the map of Atlanta as you listen. As you hear the description of each place, write the name of each place in the correct blank.

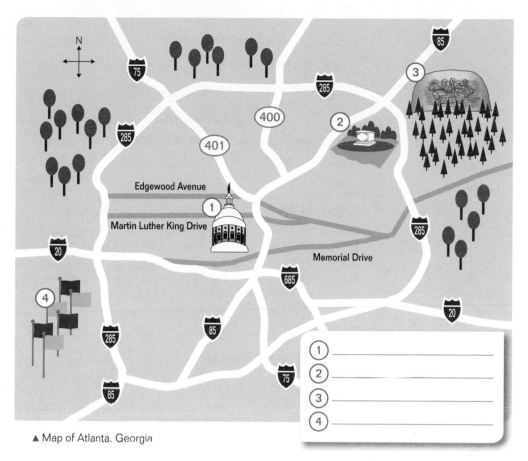

▲ Map of Atlanta, Georgia

1 _____
2 _____
3 _____
4 _____

7 Listening for Details Listen again. Write a few notes next to each location describing the location.

The Capitol Building _____
_____

Martin Luther King, Jr. National Historic Site _____
_____

Stone Mountain _____
_____

Amusement Park _____
_____

Before You Listen

8 Preparing to Listen Before you listen, discuss these questions in small groups.

1. When did you last (most recently) take a plane trip?
2. Where did you go?
3. Did you enjoy the trip? Why or why not?

9 Vocabulary Preview Listen to these words and phrases. Check (✓) the ones that you don't know.

Nouns	Verbs	Adjectives
▪ business class	▪ arrive	▪ direct
▪ economy class	▪ change planes	▪ nonrefundable
▪ first class	▪ depart	▪ nonstop
▪ one way		▪ one way (ticket)
▪ round trip		▪ round trip (ticket)

Listen

10 Listening for the Main Idea Alicia is planning a trip to Walt Disney World in Florida. She goes to a travel agency to get some information. Listen and answer this question.

How will Alicia travel? Circle the number of the correct photo.

▲ Photo 1

▼ Photo 2

11 **Listening for Specific Information** Listen again and choose the best answer to each question.

1. What kind of ticket does Alicia want to buy?

   Ⓐ first class

   Ⓑ economy class

   Ⓒ business class

2. When does Alicia's flight leave?

   Ⓐ on Saturday afternoon

   Ⓑ on Sunday evening

   Ⓒ on Sunday morning

3. Why doesn't Alicia want the nonstop, direct flight?

   Ⓐ She wants to visit Atlanta.

   Ⓑ It's much more expensive.

   Ⓒ It takes longer.

4. Why is Alicia's ticket nonrefundable?

   Ⓐ It's a special low fare.

   Ⓑ It's nonstop.

   Ⓒ She's going economy.

After You Listen

12 **Discussing Flight Information** Discuss the following questions in small groups.

1. Have you ever used a travel agent to plan a trip?

2. Which of the following would you rather do? Why?

   a. pay more for a nonstop flight (or express train) to arrive sooner

   b. pay more for a nonstop flight (or express train) so you don't have to change planes (or trains)

   c. save money by taking a longer flight (or trip) and changing planes (or trains)

3. How long in advance do you usually plan a trip?

▲ Passenger in an airplane

Planning a Trip

Asking About Flights

Helpful Questions

How much is the fare from Atlanta to. . .?
Does it make any stops?
What is the departure (or arrival) time?
How many days before the flight do I buy
the advance-purchase tickets?

Helpful Expressions

The fare is. . .
It makes . . . stop(s).
The departure (or arrival) time is. . .
There are . . . days for advance purchase.

1 **Asking About Flights** Work in small groups. Practice saying the questions and expressions in the box above. Help each other with pronunciation.

2 **Reading Flight Information**

1. Work with a partner. Student A looks at Chart A on this page.
2. Student B looks at Chart B on page 195.
3. Ask and answer questions you practiced in Activity 1.
4. Fill in the information on your charts.
5. Check your answers with your partner's chart.

Chart A					
From Atlanta to:					
City	Fare	Stops	Departure Time	Arrival Time	Advance Purchase
Chicago				12:47 P.M.	21 days
New York	$182	0	9:05 A.M.		21 days
Los Angeles	$349			1:21 P.M.	
San Francisco			9:00 A.M.		
Miami	$128	0		11:48 A.M.	
London		2	10:30 A.M.		21 days
Paris	$778			7:05 A.M.	
Tokyo			9:30 A.M.		
Vancouver		1			3 days

Chart B					
From Atlanta to:					
City	Fare	Stops	Departure Time	Arrival Time	Advance Purchase
Chicago	$118	0	9:45 A.M.		
New York				11:12 A.M.	
Los Angeles		1	9:00 A.M.		3 days
San Francisco	$349	1		1:27 P.M.	3 days
Miami			9:55 A.M.		21 days
London	$738			6:35 P.M.	
Paris		0	1:30 P.M.		7 days
Tokyo	$1,340	0		3:25 P.M.	7 days
Vancouver	$385		4:32 P.M.	9:09 P.M.	

3 Getting Trip Information Go online to get information on a trip you would like to take. Report to the class on the airfare and the times of the flights.

Discussing Travel

4 Describing Trip Destinations Work in small groups. Think of five interesting places to see in your area. Prepare a short description of each place. Tell your descriptions to the class, but don't give the names of the places. Can the class guess the places you are describing?

▲ **Student:** "This is a great place where you can get a complete view of New York City."
 Answer: Rockefeller Center

5 Talking About Travel Travel is very popular, and people like to talk about it. Pick one trip you took and tell the class something about it. Plan your talk by making notes in the chart on page 196.

Questions	Notes
What is the name of the place you went?	
Who did you go with?	
When did you go? How long did you stay?	
What did you visit?	
What special activities did you do?	
What foods did you eat?	
What was the best part of the trip?	

6 **Reading About Travel** Find a story about travel in an English-language newspaper or online. Read the story. Write three new words from the story on the lines below and their definitions. Tell the class the three new words you learned.

_____

_____

_____

_____

Self-Assessment Log

Check (✓) the words and expressions that you learned in this chapter.

Nouns
- advisory
- business class
- criminal
- economy class
- first class
- fishing equipment
- flash flood
- flat tire
- landmark
- luggage
- prison
- skyline
- sleeping bag
- spare tire
- tent
- the way back
- tower
- trunk

Verbs
- arrive
- change (a tire)
- change planes
- depart
- explore
- pull over
- should
- take up space

Adjectives
- direct
- freezing
- nonrefundable
- nonstop
- one way (ticket)
- round trip (ticket)
- triangular

Idioms and Expressions
- can't wait
- Couldn't we…
- I'd rather…
- Let's…
- Sounds good/OK
- Wouldn't you rather…

Check (✓) the things you did in this chapter. How well can you do each one?

	Very well	Fairly well	Not very well
I can listen for main ideas.	☐	☐	☐
I can listen for specific information.	☐	☐	☐
I can guess the meanings of words from context.	☐	☐	☐
I can identify stressed words and syllables.	☐	☐	☐
I can use a T-chart to compare two places.	☐	☐	☐
I can understand flight information.	☐	☐	☐
I can understand a tour guide.	☐	☐	☐
I can use my Internet search skills to find photos.	☐	☐	☐
I can persuade others.	☐	☐	☐
I can ask for travel information.	☐	☐	☐
I can talk about travel.	☐	☐	☐

Write about what you learned and what you did in this chapter.

In this chapter,

I learned _____

_____

I liked _____

_____

10 Our Planet

"Earth provides enough to satisfy every man's need but not every man's greed."

Mohandas K. Gandhi
Indian spiritual and political leader

In this
CHAPTER

Using Language
Expressing Opinions

Listening
Listening to Persuasive Messages

Speaking
Talking About Endangered Species

Connecting to the Topic

1. Describe what you see in the photo. What do you think this photo means?

2. What are some ways people can conserve energy with transportation and in the home?

3. What are some environmental problems in the world?

Earth Day

Before You Listen

1 **Prelistening Questions** Look at the following sunray graphic organizer. Discuss the questions with a classmate. Then, write on the T-chart below some of the causes of the problems and some of the solutions.

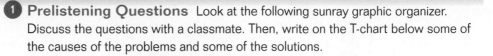

▲ Water pollution

▲ Car pollution

◀ Air pollution

1. What planet is in the center of the graphic organizer above?

2. What are some of the problems shown on the graphic organizer above?

3. What are the causes (reasons) for these problems? Fill in the "Causes of Pollution" column of the T-chart below with your partner.

4. What do you think people need to do to solve (answer) these problems? Fill in the "Solutions" column of the T-chart below.

Causes of Pollution	Solutions
Cars	Use fewer cars/more bicycles

2 **Vocabulary Preview** Lee is visiting Alicia in her dorm (dormitory) room. Listen to these words and expressions from their conversation. Check (✓) the ones that you don't know.

Nouns
- ☐ campus
- ☐ environment
- ☐ exhibit
- ☐ pollution
- ☐ student union

Verbs
- ☐ give a speech
- ☐ plant
- ☐ pollute
- ☐ support

Expression
- ☐ a lot going on

3 **Guessing the Meaning of Words** Guess the meanings of the underlined words. Write your guesses on the lines. Check your answers with a dictionary or your teacher.

1. Today the air in many cities is very dirty. Cars and factories cause this air <u>pollution</u>.

   My guess: _____

2. We live on the earth. It is our natural <u>environment</u>.

   My guess: _____

3. I'm going to <u>give a speech</u> to the class. I'm going to talk about the planet and pollution in front of the class.

   My guess: _____

4. People don't want cars and factories to <u>pollute</u> the air. We need clean, not dirty, air.

   My guess: _____

5. The Faber College <u>campus</u> is small but very nice: it has lots of outdoor places where students can study or just relax.

   My guess: _____

6. Art museums have <u>exhibits</u> of paintings or other art that people can look at.

   My guess: _____

7. Many colleges and universities have a <u>student union</u> where students can meet, get something to eat, shop, or just spend their free time.

   My guess: _____

8. I want the water and air to be clean, so I <u>support</u> Earth Day.

   My guess: _____

9. My mother's hobby is gardening: she loves to <u>plant</u> flowers and take care of them.

   My guess: _____

10. There's always <u>a lot going on</u> in a big city like London: shows, concerts, nightlife, exhibits, and other events.

    My guess: _____

4 Listening for Main Ideas Listen to the first part of the conversation. Choose the best answer to each question.

1. What is Alicia doing?
   - Ⓐ She's studying about Earth Day.
   - Ⓑ She's making a sign for Earth Day.
   - Ⓒ She's thinking about pollution.

2. On Earth Day, what do people think about?
   - Ⓐ the first Earth Day in 1970
   - Ⓑ problems with the environment
   - Ⓒ clean air and water

3. When is Earth Day?
   - Ⓐ in 1970
   - Ⓑ the last Monday in April
   - Ⓒ April 22nd

5 Listening for Specific Information (Part 1) Now listen to the whole conversation. Choose the best answer to each question.

1. What do people talk and learn about on Earth Day?
   - Ⓐ Washington, D.C.
   - Ⓑ the Earth and the environment
   - Ⓒ riding their bicycles

2. When did Earth Day start?
   - Ⓐ last year
   - Ⓑ last April 22nd
   - Ⓒ more than 30 years ago

3. What kinds of things do people think about on Earth Day?
   - Ⓐ air and pollution
   - Ⓑ clean energy
   - Ⓒ both a and b

4. What are Alicia and Lee going to do on Earth Day?
   - Ⓐ She will give a speech and he will carry a sign.
   - Ⓑ They will go to Washington, D.C.
   - Ⓒ Lee and Alicia will plant some trees.

"I'm making a sign ▶ for Earth Day."

6 Listening for Specific Information (Part 2) Listen again. Choose the best answer to each question.

1. What Earth Day activity happened one year?
   Ⓐ One thousand people came to Washington, D.C., to support pollution.
   Ⓑ People in 150 towns in Italy didn't use their cars.
   Ⓒ Students at Faber College planted trees around the student union.

2. What's going on at Faber College next Monday?
   Ⓐ There will be exhibits at the student union.
   Ⓑ Alicia will give a speech about pollution.
   Ⓒ both a and b

3. What does Lee say he wants to do on Earth Day?
   Ⓐ give a speech
   Ⓑ carry a sign
   Ⓒ plant trees

After You Listen

7 Vocabulary Review Complete the sentences below. Use words from the list.

be going on	exhibit	pollution	to plant
campus	give a speech	student union	
environment	pollute	support	

1. Cars are one of the biggest causes of air _____ .

2. After class, Beth and Ali are going to have some coffee at the

   _____.

3. I want to tell people about Earth Day, but I'm afraid to

   _____ in public.

4. Some factories _____ the air more than others.

5. Alicia and Lee _____ Earth Day because they want clean air and water.

6. What laws do we need to protect the _____ from air and water pollution?

7. The _____ at Faber College is small but very nice. It has a lot of grass and trees.

8. Many people are going _____ trees on Earth Day.

9. What will _____ in your country on Earth Day?

10. There's a special _____ about Earth Day at the local art museum.

Stress

8 **Listening for Stressed Words** Listen to the first part of the conversation again. Some of the words in the box below are stressed. Fill in the blanks with the words from the box. Some words will be used more than once.

April	fine	Monday	sign
busy	going	people	that
doing	Hi	pollution	think
Earth Day	in	problems	year
environment	is	Really	

Alicia: Come _____1_____!

Lee: _____2_____, Alicia. How's it

_____3_____?

Alicia: _____4_____, Lee. I'm _____5_____...

but _____6_____.

Lee: What are you _____7_____?

Alicia: I'm making a _____8_____ for

_____9_____.

Lee: *Earth* Day? What's _____10_____?

Alicia: On Earth Day, people _____11_____ about

_____12_____ and other _____13_____

with the _____14_____.

Lee: _____15_____! When is _____16_____?

Alicia: Next _____17_____!

Lee: ... and is it every _____18_____?

Alicia: Yes, it _____19_____. The first Earth Day was in

1970, and it now happens every _____20_____,

on _____21_____ 22nd. On _____22_____

day, _____23_____ talk and learn about

_____24_____ with the

_____25_____.

Now read the conversation with a partner. Practice stressing words.

Emphasis and Meaning

The same sentence can have different meanings if different words are emphasized or stressed. For example, listen to the following conversations.

Conversation 1

Alicia: At the student union, there will be exhibits on pollution. Students will also plant some trees around the college campus.

Lee: So what are *you* going to do on Earth Day?

Alicia: I'm going to give a speech.

Lee is asking about *Alicia's* plans compared to what other people do on Earth Day.

Conversation 2

Alicia: I usually visit my family on special days like Thanksgiving and New Year's.

Lee: So what are you going to do on *Earth Day*?

Alicia: I'm going to give a speech at the student union.

Lee is asking about Alicia's plans for *Earth Day* compared to other special days.

Conversation 3

Alicia: I think about pollution on Earth Day, and I worry about the environment.

Lee: So what are you planning to *do* on Earth Day?

Alicia: I'm going to give a speech and carry a sign.

Lee is asking about Alicia's *actions* compared to her thoughts.

9 **Listening for Emphasis** Listen to the sentences in the following conversations. Circle the letter of the sentence that you hear.

1. **a.** What do *you* think about pollution?

   b. What do you think about *pollution*?

2. **a.** Do you think *air pollution* is the biggest problem?

   b. Do you think air pollution is the *biggest* problem?

3. **a.** Will you ride your *bicycle* to school on Earth Day?

   b. Will you ride your bicycle to *school* on Earth Day?

4. **a.** How *many* trees will you plant on campus?

   b. How many trees will you plant on *campus*?

5. **a.** *Which* park are you going to clean up?

   b. Which park are *you* going to clean up?

Using the Internet

Finding News

The Internet is one of the best ways to get current news. Websites such as Yahoo! and Google have news. Newspapers and TV networks also have websites with the latest news.

To get news on the Internet, go to a site such as www.google.com and click on the News section. Then type a topic into the text box.

Example

| Everything | Images | Maps | Videos | **News** |

| Air pollution | | Submit |

10 **Practicing Your Search Skills** Look for the latest news on one of the following topics. Use the keyword and search skills that you have learned in this book. Print your news stories. Find images on your topic and bring them to class.

- Earth Day
- air or water pollution
- ways to help save the environment
- environmental organizations in your community
- celebrities (actors, musicians, etc.) who are involved in saving the environment
- your idea

Discuss your results with the class.

1. What keyword combinations did you use?
2. Did you check the URLs before you went to the site?
3. Who found the most interesting and recent stories?

Talk It Over

11 **Understanding Emphasis in Questions** Work with a partner. Look at the following conversations. Decide how Alicia would respond. Pay attention to the emphasis in Lee's questions. What information does he want? The teacher may ask you to perform your conversations for the class.

Alicia: Some people think air pollution is a big problem, but others think progress is more important.

Lee: Well, what do *you* think about pollution?

Alicia: _____

_____

Alicia: Air pollution and water pollution are two serious environmental problems.

Lee: Do you think *air pollution* is the biggest problem?

Alicia: _____

_____

Alicia: One of the things I do on Earth Day is to stop driving my car.

Lee: Will you ride your *bicycle* to school on Earth Day?

Alicia: _____

_____

Alicia: We're going to plant trees all over town on Earth Day. We have 500 trees to plant.

Lee: How many trees will you plant on *campus*?

Alicia: _____

_____

Alicia: Students from the college are going to clean up Audubon Park, Haley Park, Finley Park, and Tom Lee Park.

Lee: Which park are *you* going to clean up?

Alicia: _____

_____

PART 2 Using Language

Expressing Opinions

FOCUS

Agreeing and Disagreeing

People often have different opinions or ideas on a topic. You can have interesting conversations with people who don't agree with you. But if you give your opinion in the wrong way, people might think you are being rude. Here are some expressions to use when you agree or disagree in a conversation. Repeat them after your teacher.

To Agree	To Disagree
That's a good point.	You have a point, but…
I agree with you.	I'm afraid I don't agree with you on that.
You're right.	That may be true, but I think…
I feel the same way.	In my opinion,…
Of course,…	I understand your point of view, but…

1 **Listening for Main Ideas** Amy and Nabil are having a discussion. As you listen, answer these questions.

1. What are they talking about?
2. Do they have the same opinion, or do they disagree?

▲ Cars are one of the causes of air pollution.

2 **Listening for Opinions** Listen again. This time, pay attention to the expressions of disagreement. Circle the words you hear.

Amy: Air pollution is so bad in this city! I think the local government should stop people from driving cars on certain days.

Nabil: You (have a point / had a point). Air pollution *is* a problem, but not letting people drive on certain days is a bad idea. People need their cars to get to work, and trucks need to deliver goods to stores.

Amy: I'm afraid I (agree / don't agree) with you there. Saving the environment is (so / too) important. People are so used to driving that they don't think of other ways to do things. If we stopped people from driving on certain days, maybe we could think of new ways to get around.

Nabil: I understand (you / your point of view), but I still think it wouldn't be possible to stop people from driving.

3 Debating

1. As a class, choose a topic from the chart below and divide into two teams. Your teacher will help you decide which side of the topic your team will debate.

2. Line up chairs in two facing rows as in the picture.

Side A   **Side B**

3. First a student on one side states an opinion for his or her team.

4. Then a student on the other side states an opinion. Use the expressions of agreement and disagreement. Continue until each student has had a turn.

5. Your teacher will give a point to each student who uses one of the expressions. The team with the most points at the end wins.

Topics	
Side A	**Side B**
The government should *not* permit people to drive cars in cities.	The government *should* permit people to drive cars in cities.
The government should permit parents to have *more than one* child.	The government should permit parents to have *only one* child.
Students should *only* study in school; they *shouldn't* play sports.	Students *need* sports in school; they *should do more than* only study.
People *should* be able to smoke in public places such as restaurants.	People *should not* be able to smoke in public places such as restaurants.

▲ Students should not play sports in school. They should only study.

▲ Students need sports. They should play sports in school.

Getting Meaning from Context

1 Using Context Clues You will hear five speakers. Listen to each speaker. Write the number of the speaker next to the best answer below. Continue to listen to check each answer.

_____ air pollution

_____ crime

_____ water pollution

_____ overcrowding (too many people)

_____ the environment

Listening to Persuasive Messages

Before You Listen

2 Preparing to Listen Before you listen, discuss these questions in a small group.

1. What do people do in their everyday lives to contribute to pollution and other environmental problems?

2. Do you personally do anything to help the environment?

3 Vocabulary Preview Listen to these words and phrases. Check (✓) the ones that you don't know.

Nouns
- carbon dioxide
- endangered species
- faucet
- recyclables
- shuttle bus
- topsoil
- toxic chemicals

Verb
- recycle

Adjectives
- mature
- slaughtered
- veggie (vegetable)

Listen

4 Listening for the Main Idea (Part 1) Listen to the following messages. As you listen, answer this question.

Where might you hear these messages?

5 Listening for Main Ideas (Part 2) Listen again. This time, write the number of the message next to the main idea of the message.

a. _____ Save water.

b. _____ Don't eat meat.

c. _____ Don't drive your car.

d. _____ Recycle—don't throw things away.

e. _____ Eat food without chemicals.

6 Listening for Details Listen again. This time, match each of the main messages with the details about how you can help or hurt the environment. There may be more than one detail for each main message.

Main Message	**Details**
1. Save water. _____	**a.** Raising cattle for meat uses a lot of water, topsoil, and other resources.
	b. It's better to recycle your trash than to throw it away.
2. Don't eat meat. _____	**c.** Cars pollute the air.
	d. Animals raised for meat contain toxic chemicals.
3. Don't drive your car. _____	**e.** Trees produce oxygen to replace polluted air.
	f. Raising cattle for meat adds carbon dioxide to the air.
4. Recycle, don't throw things away. _____	**g.** Turn the water off while you brush your teeth.
	h. Burgers made from vegetables are better for the environment than burgers made from meat.
5. Eat food without chemicals. _____	**i.** Chemicals used to kill bugs on vegetables can cause cancer.
	j. Cars cause noise pollution on city streets.

After You Listen

7 **Discussing Main Ideas** Answer these questions in small groups.

1. Do you agree with any of the main messages from the announcements at the Earth Fair? Which ones?

2. If you disagree with any of the main messages, tell your group why you disagree.

3. Do the members of your group do anything to help the environment? On the chart, list what actions you do in each of the following areas.

Goals	Actions Your Group Takes
1. Reduce air pollution from cars	
2. Save water	
3. Recycle glass, paper, cans, etc.	
4. Reduce use of toxic chemicals	
5. Reduce air travel	
6. Shop at farmer's markets	
7. Other environmental issues	

Talking About Endangered Species

1 **Reading About Endangered Species** Read the passage below.

The Endangered Species List

Since the year 1600, more than 100 different kinds of animals have become extinct. That is, those animals don't exist anymore. We will never see another of those animals alive. Many more types of animals will disappear if they are not saved. These animals are called "endangered species."

▲ An American grizzly bear, no longer endangered

Endangered species are protected from hunting and other threats. Sometimes, animals are taken off the endangered species list because they have become more numerous. The American grizzly bear is one example of success.

2 Locating Endangered Species on a Map

1. Work with a partner. Decide which one of you is Student A and which is Student B.

2. Student A should look at Map A on page 214. Student B should look at Map B on page 215.

3. Each map indicates a different endangered species. Ask your partner questions and write in the missing information on the lines of your map. When you are finished, check your maps.

Example

Student A (looking at Map A): What animal is endangered in North America?

Student B (looking at Map B): The American alligator.

Map A

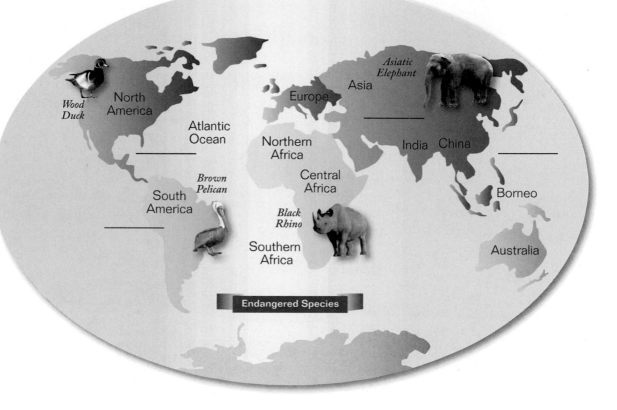

Map B

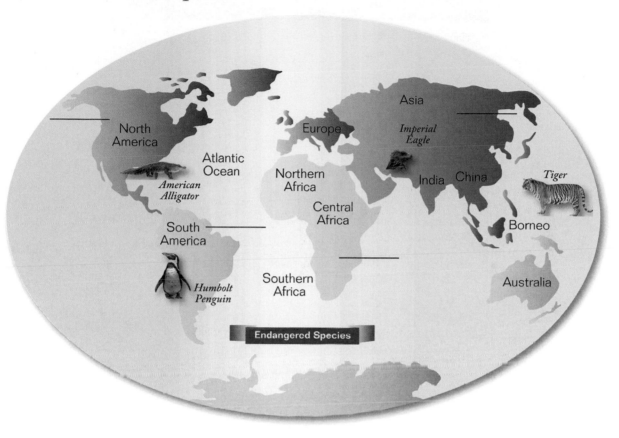

North America

Atlantic Ocean

American Alligator

South America

Humbolt Penguin

Europe

Northern Africa

Central Africa

Southern Africa

Asia

Imperial Eagle

India   China

Tiger

Borneo

Australia

Endangered Species

3 **Discussing Endangered Species** There are many reasons why animals are endangered. The chart below shows some of the reasons. Work in small groups. Decide which animals on Maps A and B are disappearing and for which reasons. Write the name of each animal beside its reason. There may be more than one reason for some animals. Discuss your answers with the class.

Reasons	Animals
Hunted by humans for food	
Hunted by humans for furs, feathers, tusks, etc.	
Captured and sold as pets	
Without a place to live after people cut down the forests	
Dying because of air and water pollution	
Dying because of other human activity	

4 **Researching Endangered Species** Visit the World Wildlife Organization at www.worldwildlife.org. Answer the questions.

1. Search by area of the world. What species are endangered in your area?

2. Find information to fill out the following chart. Report your results to the class.

Animal	Reason for Endangerment	What People are Doing to Solve the Problem

Self-Assessment Log

Check (✓) the words and expressions that you learned in this chapter.

Nouns
- campus
- carbon dioxide
- endangered species
- environment
- exhibit
- faucet
- pollution
- recyclables
- shuttle bus

- student union
- topsoil
- toxic chemicals

Verbs
- give a speech
- plant
- pollute
- recycle
- support

Adjectives
- mature
- slaughtered
- veggie (vegetable)

Expression
- a lot going on

Check (✓) the things you did in this chapter. How well can you do each one?

	Very well	Fairly well	Not very well
I can listen for main ideas.	☐	☐	☐
I can listen for specific information.	☐	☐	☐
I can guess the meanings of words from context.	☐	☐	☐
I can identify and use stress and emphasis.	☐	☐	☐
I can listen for emphasis to understand meaning.	☐	☐	☐
I can use expressions to tell my opinion.	☐	☐	☐
I can participate in a debate.	☐	☐	☐
I can use the Internet to find current news.	☐	☐	☐
I can talk about the environment and endangered species.	☐	☐	☐

Write about what you learned and what you did in this chapter.

In this chapter,

I learned _____

_____

I liked _____

_____

Audioscript

CHAPTER 1

Neighborhoods, Cities, and Towns

PART 1   Where Are You From?

④ **Listening for Main Ideas** page 6

⑤ **Listening for Specific Information** page 6

⑦ **Listening for Stressed Words** page 8

⑧ **Marking Stressed Words** page 8

Alex: Hello everyone. Welcome to Faber College Webcast. My name is Alex. Today, I'm talking to three new students at Faber. So, where are you from?

Ali: I'm from Silver Spring, Maryland.

Alex: Wow! That's near a big city—Washington, D.C.

Lee: And I'm from Seoul, Korea.

Alex: That's a big city, too. Faber is in a small town. How do you feel about living here?

Lee: I'm excited. I like the campus. It's pretty and quiet. There are so many trees!

Alex: What about you, Ali? Are you excited?

Ali: Not really. In fact, I'm a little nervous. This is my first time away from home.

Alex: That's very normal. A lot of students feel nervous at first. Now, Beth, you're from a small town, right?

Beth: Yes. I come from San Anselmo. It's a small town in Northern California.

Alex: What's it like?

Beth: Well, it's a lot like this town, so I'm very comfortable here.

Alex: Great! Now, a lot of new students miss their friends from home. What about you?

Ali: Yeah, I really miss my friends.

Beth: I miss my friends, too, Ali, but there's a lot to do at Faber College—sports, clubs…

Lee: Yes, campus activities are a good way to meet people.

Ali: Hmm… That sounds like a great idea!

Alex: Well, our time is up. Thank you, Ali, Lee, and Beth. We hope you enjoy your time here at Faber College.

⑩ **Listening for Contractions** page 9

1. There're a lot of activities on campus.

2. She is from a small town.

3. What is your name?

4. It's noisy here!

5. I'm from Silver Spring.

6. San Anselmo is a small town.

7. There is a lot of noise in here.

8. He's from New York City.

PART 2   Using Language

① **Listening for Contact Information** page 14

Conversation 1

Ms. Dunn: Student Advising. May I help you?

Michael Green: Uh, yes, I'm a new student. I'd like to make an appointment to talk with an advisor.

Ms. Dunn: Sure. First, I need a little information. What's your name?

Michael Green: Michael Green. That's M-I-C-H-A-E-L G-R-E-E-N.

Ms. Dunn: And what is your address?

Michael Green: I live at 3467 Grand Avenue, Apartment 7.

Ms. Dunn: That's 3467 Grand Avenue, Apartment 7?

Michael Green: That's right.

Ms. Dunn: What is your phone number?

Michael Green: My number is area code 301-555-5634.

Ms. Dunn: 301-555-5634?

Michael Green: That's right.

Conversation 2

Mr. Brown: So, you want the college to send you your grades?

Lara Li: Yes, please.

Mr. Brown: OK. What's your name?

Lara Li: My name is Lara Li.

Mr. Brown: Is that L-E-E?

Lara Li: No, it's L-I.

Mr. Brown: And how do you spell your first name?

Lara Li: It's L-A-R-A.

Mr. Brown: And your address?

Lara Li: It's P.O. Box 678, Brooklyn, New York, 11215.

Mr. Brown: And do you have an email address? That's in case we have any questions.

Lara Li: Of course. It's lara li @ ials.com

Mr. Brown: Thanks.

Conversation 3

Call center employee: What is your name?

Ana Martinez: Ana Martinez. A-N-A M-A-R-T-I-N-E-Z.

Employee: And where shall I send this?

Ana Martinez: 456 Oak Street, Los Angeles, California, 91344.

Employee: What's your telephone number?

Ana Martinez: Why do you need it?

Employee: In case we have a question about your order.

Ana Martinez: OK. It's 213-555-3497.

Employee: OK. And what is your email address?

Ana Martinez: Sorry. I don't give out my email address to companies.

Employee: That's OK. We'll send this out today.

Conversation 4

Rick: Hey there. What's your name?

Marta: Uhh… Marta.

Rick: Uh, Marta what?

Marta: I'd rather not say.

Rick: So, anyway, Marta, can I call or text you sometime?

Marta: Sorry, I don't give out my phone number.

PART 3 Listening

2 Using Context Clues page 17

Conversation 1

Beth: Sara, this is my friend Lee.

Sara: Hi, Lee. Nice to meet you.

Lee: Nice to meet you, too. Are you a student at Faber College?

Sara: No, I go to the University of California.

Lee: The University of California? What's it like?

Sara: It's not at all like Faber College. It's huge. There are over 40,000 students.

Question 1. *What is the University of California like?*

Lee: Wow! That's a lot of students!

Sara: Yes, but I have a lot of friends there.

Conversation 2

Ali: So, how do you like Faber College?

Alicia: I like it a lot. There's a lot to do, and my classes are interesting.

Ali: What classes are you taking?

Alicia: I'm taking Statistics, Contemporary English Literature, and Introduction to Networking. How about you?

Ali: I'm taking Contemporary English Lit and Statistics, too. I'm also taking History of American Art.

Alicia: So what's your favorite class?

Ali: Well, English and Statistics are hard… but I really enjoy Art History.

Question 2. *What does Ali think about his Art History class?*

Alicia: Art History? What do you like about that class?

Ali: Well, it's interesting, and it's fun. And the best thing is that it's not hard at all like my other classes.

Conversation 3

Alex: So, do you want to get some lunch at the café?

Beth: Sure, but I need to get some money first.

Alex: Are you going to the bank?

Beth: No, I'm just looking for an ATM.

Alex: There are a few ATMs on campus. There's one in the Student Union and there's one next to the gym.

Beth: Which one is closer?

Alex: The one in the Student Union.

Question 3. *Where is Beth going?*

Beth: Let's go to that ATM, then. I don't want to walk too far. And we can go to the café afterwards.

Conversation 4

Jamie: Can I help you?

Lee: Yes. I'm looking for the English Department.

Jamie: Oh, that's on the other side of campus.

Lee: How do I get there?

Jamie: Just go straight ahead. Pass the Student Union.

Lee: Uh-huh.

Jamie: And turn right at the café…

Lee: Turn right at the café… OK.

Jamie: Next to the café is the library.

Lee: OK.

Jamie: Walk past the library and there you are. It's the next building.

Question 4. *Where is the English Department?*

Lee: Right next door?

Jamie: Yep. It's right across from the gym. You can't miss it.

Conversation 5

Beth: So how do you get to school every day?

Lee: I take the bus. It's crowded, but it's fast. And the bus stop is near my apartment. How about you?

Beth: Yeah, the bus stop is near my place, too. But I walk.

Lee: Gee, you live far from campus. That must take a long time. Why do you walk?

Beth: It's healthy. I don't have time to go to the gym, and we sit all day in class.

Question 5. *Why doesn't Beth take the bus?*

Lee: Yeah, I guess you're right.

Beth: Yeah, walking for 45 minutes is a lot healthier than sitting on the bus!

5 **Listening for the Main Idea** page 19

6 **Listening for Details** page 19

Man: So you live in the South Beach neighborhood?

Woman: Yes. It's an exciting neighborhood. People from all over the world live there.

Man: What do you like about it?

Woman: There are a lot of ethnic restaurants and shops. You can get things from all over the world in South Beach. There are cafés and movie theaters, too.

Man: What about public transportation?

Woman: There are a lot of bus stops on my street, and there's a subway station right on my block. It's very convenient.

Man: But it's kind of noisy there, right?

Woman: Right. It isn't quiet, especially at night. And there's a lot of traffic, too. How about you? What neighborhood do you live in?

Man: I live in Little Gables.

Woman: What's that like?

Man: It's quiet and peaceful. There are a lot of trees. There's a big park at the end of my block.

Woman: Do you know your neighbors?

Man: Yes. Everyone's friendly and helpful.

Woman: Sounds very nice!

Man: Yes, but it's a little boring. There isn't much to do. And there isn't good transportation. I have to drive everywhere.

Woman: Hmm… I think I'll stay in South Beach!

9 **Listening for the Main Idea** page 21

10 **Listening for Specific Information** page 21

11 **Checking Directions** page 21

Man: Excuse me. How do I get to the California Film Institute from here?

Woman: Umm… Go up this street for two blocks. Then turn left on A Street. Oh, wait a minute. I mean turn *right* on A Street. Yes, right. OK. Stay on A for two blocks. Then when you get to 3rd Street… uhm, no, I mean 4th Street, turn right. Uhm, turn right on 4th Street. As soon as you turn right, go just a short way. The theater is on your right. You can't miss it. It's next to the Starbucks.

Man: Got it! Thanks!

PART 1 Conversation: Shopping

5 **Listening for Main Ideas (Part 1)** page 30

6 **Listening for Main Ideas (Part 2)** page 31

7 **Listening for Specific Information** page 31

10 **Listening for Stressed Words** page 33

Alicia: Hi, Beth. Come on in.

Beth: Hi, Alicia! How are you doing?

Alicia: Pretty good.

Beth: Alicia, this is my friend Ali. He's from Silver Spring, Maryland.

Alicia: Hi, Ali. It's nice to meet you.

Ali: Nice to meet you, too.

Alicia: Well, please come in and have a seat!

Beth, Ali: Thanks!

Alicia: Can I get you something? Coffee? Soda?

Beth: Oh, no thanks.

Ali: No thank you. I'm fine.

Beth: So, Alicia, we're going to go shopping. Do you want to come?

Alicia: Gee, I don't know… I shop mostly online these days.

Ali: Really? Why is that?

Alicia: Because it saves time—and gas!

Ali: Oh, right!

Beth: What do you mean?

Ali: Well, you don't have to drive your car . . .

Alicia: Right. And you don't have to look for parking. The mall is so crowded these days.

Beth: Yeah, but online, you can't see things very well. And you can't touch them! And, with clothes, you can't try them on! I like to browse when I go shopping!

Ali: Me, too!… and it's such a nice day… why do you want to sit in front of a computer screen?

Alicia: Yeah, I see what you mean… but I don't have much money!

Beth: No problem! You can come with us and save money.

Alicia: How?

Beth: We aren't going to take any money or credit cards with us. And we aren't going to spend any money. We're just going to look around.

Ali: That's right! We're going *window*-shopping.

Alicia: Great idea! Then I *am* going!

⑫ Listening for Reductions page 34

1. It's nice to meetchya.
2. Arencha comin'?
3. I'm spending too much money.
4. Do you want to go shopping?
5. Do you hafta study today?

PART 2   Using Language

❶ Listening for Reasons page 37

❷ Listening for Specific Information page 38

Clerk: May I help you?

Customer: Yes. I'd like to return this sweater.

Clerk: OK. Why are you returning the sweater?

Customer: Because it's not the right size.

Clerk: Do you have your receipt?

Customer: Yes. Here it is.

Clerk: OK. I need your name, please.

Customer: My name is Anna McGuire.

Clerk: And your address?

Customer: It's 452 West Hammond Street.

Clerk: OK. Here you go: $43.95.

Customer: Thank you!

PART 3   Listening

❶ Using Context Clues page 39

Conversation 1

Beth: Wow! This is a really big mall!

Alicia: Yeah, it is. Hey, I think I want to spend some money after all!

Ali: Well, maybe there's a bank here.

Beth: No, she doesn't need a bank. She can just use that machine over there.

Alicia: Oh, yeah… Let's see if I have my card.

Ali: How much are you gonna take out?

Alicia: Oh, maybe $200.

Question 1. *What are Ali, Alicia, and Beth talking about?*

Ali: So, what's that called in English—a change machine?

Alicia: No, it's an automated teller, right?

Beth: Yeah. Or ATM for Automated Teller Machine.

Ali: Wait a minute, have you forgotten? We aren't going to need that. We're saving our money, right? Let's just keep window-shopping.

Conversation 2

Ali: Hey! Let's go in here! Look at all that great equipment!

Beth: Uh-oh, Alicia! Ali loves soccer and baseball. He's going to want to do more than window-shopping in this store.

Alicia: I think you're right. C'mon, Ali. You're not going in there, are you?

Question 2. *What shop are Ali, Alicia, and Beth standing in front of now?*

Ali: C'mon, just for a minute. I really love sports.

Alicia: Yes, but we're supposed to be window-shopping. Besides, mmm! Can you smell that?

Ali and Beth: Yeah!

Conversation 3

Beth: Fresh chocolate chip cookies!

Alicia: And brownies!

Ali: It all smells delicious. But we don't have any money, remember?

Alicia: Well, I do have about $4.

Ali: OK, let's go in!

Question 3. *Where are they going now?*

Beth: Wow! What a great bakery! I'll have one chocolate chip cookie.

Alicia: They're $1.50 each, three for $4. We have just enough.

Ali: Thanks, Alicia. Mmm!

Conversation 4

Ali: Where to now?

Beth: How about across the way? We can spend a few minutes looking at the new magazines and best sellers.

Alicia: Well, if you really want to. But I don't really like English magazines.

Ali: I'll bet they have Spanish magazines.

Question 4. *Where are Ali and Beth going to go next?*

Alicia: Nah, you two go to the bookstore. I'm going somewhere else.

Conversation 5

Beth: All right, Alicia. Then let's meet in front of the elevators in half an hour—at one o'clock, OK?

Alicia: OK. I'm going to look at some sweaters and boots. It's getting cold, you know.

Ali and Beth: OK.

Question 5. *Where is Alicia going?*

Alicia: Oh, Beth. Isn't there a good clothing store on the first floor?

Beth: Yes, there is. Go down those stairs and turn right.

4 Listening for the Main Idea page 40

5 Listening for Store Names page 41

6 Listening for Prices page 42

7 Listening to Compare Prices page 43

Ad 1

Are you looking for a great pair of jeans? How about Wild West jeans? Cost Club has Wild West blue jeans for only $29.99 a pair—the lowest price in town!

Ad 2

Get the best price on Wild West blue jeans at Larson's Discount House. Larson's has your favorite jeans for only $31.99. That's right... only $31.99! Hurry, before...

Ad 3

Morton's Department Store is having its Big Spring Sale! All your favorite brands are on sale now. Just listen to these prices: Wild West jeans for only $35.99! Spring Step...

11 Listening for the Main Idea page 44

12 Listening to Online Shopping Information page 44

SuperMall22.com

Online shoppers now have a special place to buy everything they need: SuperMall22 .com. SuperMall22.com is a shopping website, but it's different from other online shopping sites. First of all, you can buy *anything* at SuperMall22.com. No more going to one site for food, another for gifts, and another for furniture. SuperMall22.com offers everything from groceries to clothes to refrigerators, all at one website, and all in one transaction. And no more filling out several different online forms with your credit card and shipping information. Another big difference is that SuperMall22.com promises to deliver your purchases one day after you place your order. Now that's really saving time...

PART 1 Conversation:
Staying in Touch

5 **Listening for Main Ideas** page 53

6 **Listening for Specific Information (Part 1)** page 54

7 **Listening for Specific Information (Part 2)** page 55

9 **Listening for Stressed Words** page 56

10 **Marking Stressed Words** page 56

Beth: What are you doing, Ali?

Ali: I'm on Facebook.

Lee: Are you posting something? Or just reading?

Ali: I'm reading some posts from my friends back home. I like to see what they are doing.

Beth: I like to get updates, too. Facebook is a good way to keep in touch with friends.

Lee: Is your family on Facebook, too?

Ali: My sister is. She often posts pictures of her baby. It's fun to see him grow up. But my parents don't want to use social media.

Beth: Do they have email?

Ali: Yes, I can stay in touch with them by email or by texting, but I also call them once a week. I often call my sister in London, too.

Lee: Do you have international calling on your cell phone?

Beth: I do, but it's very expensive.

Ali: I use Skype on the computer. I can call them for free that way.

Lee: So, you don't have to pay? I'm going to try that! Can you see the baby online when you call?

Ali: Yes. I can watch him play, and he talks a little.

Beth: Wow! Technology is amazing, isn't it?

Lee: It sure is!

12 **Listening for Reductions** page 56

1. What are ya doin' ?
2. I like to see what they're doing.
3. They don't want to use it.
4. I can call 'em for free.
5. I am going to try that.

PART 2 Using Language

2 **Listening for Conversation Starters** page 60

3 **Listening for Details** page 61

Conversation 1:

Speaker 1: Excuse me. Can you help me?

Speaker 2: Of course. What do you need?

Speaker 1: Do you have this shirt in blue?

Speaker 2: No. It comes in white and green. Would you like the white one?

Speaker 1: Yes, I would.

Conversation 2:

Speaker 1: Hi, Ben. How are you doing?

Speaker 2: Hi, Chris. I'm fine. Have you met my sister Ann?

Speaker 1: No. It's nice to meet you, Ann. Do you live here, too?

Speaker 3: No. I live with my mother and father. I'm just visiting Ben.

Conversation 3:

Speaker 1: Excuse me. Can you answer a question for us?

Speaker 2: Certainly, if I can.

Speaker 3: How do we get to the park from here?

Speaker 2: Go straight down this road, and turn right at the post office.

Speaker 1: Thank you so much!

PART 3   Listening

1 **Using Context Clues** page 63

Conversation 1

Ali: What are you doing, Beth?

Beth: Do you remember the party last week?

Ali: Sure. We had a great time!

Beth: I took some good photos. I want my Facebook friends to see all the fun.

Question 1. *What is Beth doing?*

Conversation 2

Ali: The bookstore has a special sale on t-shirts today.

Lee: Really? How much are they?

Ali: If you buy one for $12, you get one for free.

Lee: That's a great deal!

Ali: Yes, I got 4 t-shirts.

Question 2.
How much did Ali pay for his t-shirts?

Conversation 3

Beth: Ali, come with us. We're going to the gym.

Ali: I can't. I always call my parents on Sunday afternoons.

Lee: Every Sunday?

Ali: Yes. My sister is at their house on Sundays, so I can talk to everyone.

Question 3.
How often does Ali call his parents?

Conversation 4

Lee: Ali, look at the sky over there.

Ali: Wow. It's all red with purple streaks.

Lee: What a beautiful sunset! It's amazing, isn't it?

Ali: It sure is!

Question 4.
What does Ali think about the sunset?

Conversation 5

Alicia: Beth, do you want to go to the mall with me?

Beth: Sure. Why are you going to the mall?

Alicia: It's my brother's birthday next week. I have to get a birthday card.

Beth: Do you have to get him a present, too?

Alicia: He told me not to spend a lot of money on him.

Question 5.
What is Alicia going to get at the mall?

4 **Listening for the Main Idea** page 64

5 **Listening to Voicemail** page 64

Message 1: Dan? This is Joe Adams at the International Students' Office. I have a form that I need you to sign. Can you come by my office some time tomorrow? If not, call me back on my cell. 555-678-2215.

Message 2: This is Professor Davis. I got your message. I'd be happy to talk to you about the assignment. Please come to my office Thursday at 3:00. I look forward to seeing you then.

Message 3: Hi. This is Suzie Scott. Remember me from your history class? I'd like to get together with you for coffee someday next week. Call me back. If I'm in class, you can leave a message.

Message 4: Hey, buddy! How are you doing? I'm going to the library. Meet me there, and we can study for the test.

9 **Listening for the Main Idea** page 66

10 **Listening to Descriptions of People** page 66

Speaker: Alicia is a typical college student. Where do I begin? She is not too heavy and she is not too thin. She is not too short and she is not too tall. She wears the perfect clothes for fall. Her hair is straight and light brown. She's a medium-sized girl—just right!

PART 1 Conversation:
Calling a Hospital

4 **Listening for Main Ideas (Part 1)**
page 74

5 **Listening for Main Ideas (Part 2)**
page 74

6 **Listening for Specific Information**
page 75

8 **Listening for Stressed Words** page 76

Recording:	Welcome to Faber Hospital and Clinics. If this is an emergency, please hang up and call 9-1-1. Please listen carefully as our menu options have changed. For the 24-hour pharmacy, please press 1. For Family Medicine, press 2. For the health clinic, press 3. To speak to the operator, please press 0 or just stay on the line.
Ali (thinking):	Hmm. I need the clinic; I'll press 3.
Receptionist:	Health Clinic. Can I help you?
Ali:	Yes. I think I have the flu. I feel awful.
Receptionist:	Would you like to make an appointment?
Ali:	Yes, I'd like to see a doctor.
Receptionist:	All right. Could you come in tomorrow afternoon at one o'clock?
Ali:	Yes, I can come by then. Oh! Should I bring any money?
Receptionist:	No—just your ID and insurance card.
Ali:	OK.
Receptionist:	Now, could I have your name and insurance number?
Ali:	Yes. My family name is Halal, H-A-L-A-L. My first name is Ali, A-L-I. And my insurance number is 000-481-624.
Receptionist:	OK. You're all set. Don't forget to bring your health insurance card when you come in tomorrow.
Ali:	OK.
Receptionist:	All right, we'll see you tomorrow at one.
Ali:	Yes, thank you… thank you very much. Bye.
Receptionist:	Bye.

10 **Listening for Reductions** page 77

1. C'n I help you?
2. Would you like to make an appointment?
3. Cudja come in tomorrow afternoon at one?
4. No—just your ID and insurance card.

PART 2 Using Language

2 **Listening for Main Ideas** page 80

3 **Listening for Specific Information**
page 80

Ramona:	I had an argument with Sue. Now she won't talk to me. What should I do?
Rick:	Well, Ramona, she's probably angry with you right now. Maybe that's why she doesn't want to talk to you.
Ramona:	Yeah, you're right.
Rick:	I think you should write her a very nice letter. Tell her that you still want to be friends.
Ramona:	OK. Then what?
Rick:	You should wait a week, and then call her again. Maybe then she'll talk to you.
Ramona:	That's good advice. Thanks, Rick.

2 **Using Context Clues** page 82

Call 1

Caller 1: Yes. I'd like to make an appointment.

Man: What seems to be the problem?

Caller 1: I've got a really bad headache.

Man: Did you take your temperature?

Caller 1: No, but I think I've got a fever. My head feels warm.

Man: Hmm. Sounds like the flu. When can you come in?

Question 1:
Who is the woman probably calling?

Man: Health clinic. May I help you?

Caller 1: Yes. I'd like to make an appointment.

Call 2

Caller 2 : Hello. I'd like to report a stolen bicycle.

Man: May I have your name, please?

Caller 2: The last name is Chavez, C-H-A-V-E-Z. First name, Maria, M-A-R-I-A.

Man: Address?

Caller 2: 121 High Street, Apartment 3B.

Man: And where was the bike stolen from?

Caller 2: In front of my apartment building. It was…

Question 2:
Who is the woman probably calling?

Man: Police Department. Officer Wyman speaking.

Caller 2: Hello. I'd like to report a stolen bicycle.

Call 3

Caller 3: Hi. My name's Beth Johnston. I'd like to make an appointment.

Man: All right, Beth. Is this for a checkup or a cleaning?

Caller 3: A checkup. I think I have a bad cavity. The side of my head hurts.

Man: Which tooth hurts?

Caller 3: One of the back ones.

Man: Let me see… We can see you this afternoon if you can come in at 4:30.

Question 3: *Who is the speaker calling?*

Man: Dental clinic. This is Mr. Adams.

Caller 3: Hi. My name's Beth Johnston. I'd like to make an appointment.

Call 4

Caller 4: Please! You must help me! My apartment's on fire!

Woman: Please try to stay calm, sir. Where is the fire?

Caller 4: There's smoke everywhere.

Woman: Excuse me… are you out of the apartment?

Caller 4: Yes, I am! Please send help immediately!

Woman: Now, sir, stay calm. Where are you located?

Question 4: *Who is the man probably calling?*

Woman: Fire Department.

Caller 4: Please! You must help me! My apartment's on fire!

Call 5

Caller 5: Yes, I'd like to make an appointment.

Man: Have you ever been here before?

Caller 5: No, but I'm a student, and all of a sudden, I can't see things on the board in the front of the classroom very well…

Man: OK. It sounds like you need an exam.

Caller 5: Great. I've been so worried…

Question 5: *Who is the speaker calling?*

Man: Eye clinic. This is Sean.

Caller 5: Yes, I'd like to make an appointment.

⑤ Listening for the Main Idea page 82

⑥ Listening to Instructions page 83

Ali: I feel like I have a very bad cold. I have a fever, I ache all over, and I cough and sneeze all the time.

Dr. Dirks: You probably have the flu, or influenza. It's much more serious than a cold. You have to take care of yourself, or you could become very sick. You should stay in bed and rest as much as possible. You can take two aspirin, four times a day. That will help the fever and the aches and pains. Be sure to drink plenty of fluids. Fruit juice and hot tea are the best. Here's a prescription for some cough medicine. You can take it to any drugstore. Be sure to take your medicine with your meals because it might upset your stomach.

Ali: I understand. Thanks.

⑩ Listening for Main Ideas page 85

⑪ Listening for Specific Information page 85

Number 1

Speaker 1: I have a terrible headache. The pain is right at the back of my head. It seems to go from ear to ear.

Number 2

Speaker 2: I think I have the flu. I vomited twice after breakfast this morning. I guess I shouldn't eat anything.

Number 3

Speaker 3: I was playing soccer and fell over another player. Now I can't stand up or walk. I think I broke my leg.

Number 4

Speaker 4: I just had a drink with ice, and now my tooth really hurts—here on the right side of my mouth. I must have a cavity.

Number 5

Speaker 5: I tripped on the curb when crossing the street and twisted my ankle. I can walk, but it really hurts. I think I sprained it.

Number 6

Speaker 6: I don't feel too bad, but I kept sneezing and coughing in class today. I knew there was a cold going around, but I didn't think I would catch it.

CHAPTER 5 Men and Women

PART 1 Conversation: Making Connections At School

④ Listening for Main Ideas (Part 1) page 94

⑤ Listening for Main Ideas (Part 2) page 94

⑥ Listening for Specific Information page 94

⑧ Listening for Stressed Words page 96

Alex: Welcome to another Faber College webcast! My name is Alex. Today, we're talking about making connections on campus. Let me introduce three students we met a few weeks ago: Beth …

Beth: Hi, Alex.

Alex: Ali…

Ali: Nice to see you again!

Alex: You, too!… and Lee.

Lee: Hi, Alex!

Alex: So, let's start with you, Lee. You just joined the Faber College soccer team, didn't you?

Lee: Well, no, Alex. I'm not that good a soccer player but I am playing intramural soccer.

Alex:	Great!... and do you like it?
Lee:	I sure do! It's great exercise and a great way to meet people.
Alex:	... and how about you, Ali?
Ali:	I just joined the International Dance Club.
Alex:	That sounds like fun! Is it?
Ali:	It sure is! I'm learning dances from around the world.
Alex:	And I'm sure it's a great way to meet women, too, right?
Ali:	Well,... yeah,... it is!
Alex:	Now, Beth, what about you?
Beth:	I'm a member of the Language Exchange Club.
Alex:	And what's that all about?
Beth:	Well, I meet once or twice a week with my conversation partner, Michel. He's from France.
Alex:	So, you help Michel with English?
Beth:	That's right. And he helps me in French. It's a great way to practice a language. I met him through the club.
Alex:	I'm sure it is . . . and a great way for men and women to meet each other, right?
Beth:	Maybe, but... I'd rather not say!
Alex:	OK, OK! Thank you, everyone. Well, that's our webcast for today. Remember Faber College students: join a club or group. It's a great way to meet people and make connections!

10 Listening for Reductions   page 97

1. What ja do last weekend?
2. Why did you join the Dance Club?
3. How did you make connections at your school?
4. Who ja meet in the Language Exchange Club?
5. When ju get here?

PART 2   Using Language

2 Listening to Small Talk   page 101

Small-talk conversation 1

Man 1:	Beautiful day for the game, isn't it?
Man 2:	Yes, it is! Are you a Dodger's fan?
Man 1:	I sure am! I hope they beat the Yankees!

Small-talk conversation 2

Woman 1:	This place is nice and quiet, isn't it?
Woman 2:	It sure is, and the sushi is great!
Woman 1:	Yes, it is.

Small-talk conversation 3

Man:	This is going to be a great show! What do you think?
Woman:	Yes, I think so, too! I'm a big Celine Dion fan!
Man:	Me, too. I love her singing.

Small-talk conversation 4

Man:	Excuse me. Is this the line for the sandwiches?
Woman:	Yes, it is.
Man:	Thanks. I'm new here. Is the cafeteria food any good?
Woman:	Yeah, usually. But don't try the coffee— it's terrible!
Man:	Ha ha! OK, I won't!... I'm Brad, by the way.
Woman:	Hi Brad. I'm Sharon. Nice to meet you.
Man:	You, too. So, do you usually have lunch in the cafeteria?

PART 3   Listening

2 Using Context Clues   page 104

Conversation 1

Alicia:	Hi, Beth! What are you doing?
Beth:	I'm reading a text message from Michel.
Alicia:	Michel's your language partner in the Language Exchange Club, isn't he?

Beth: Yes, he is.

Alicia: So, does he want to meet for more language practice?

Beth: Well, not really… He's asking if I want to have dinner with him this Friday night.

Question 1. *What is Michel asking Beth?*

Alicia: You mean, he's asking you out on a date?

Beth: He sure is!

Conversation 2

Beth: So, Alicia, can I ask you something?

Alicia: Sure! What?

Beth: Well, I like Michel, but maybe I shouldn't go out with him. Maybe I should just practice French with him…

Alicia: What's the problem if you like him?

Beth: I'm not sure. I'm American and he's French, so…

Alicia: So what?

Question 2. *How does Alicia probably feel about Beth going out with Michel?*

Alicia: Look, Beth, if you like Michel, it's not important where you come from or where he comes from. Go out with him! Have fun!

Beth: You're right, Alicia. Thanks!

Conversation 3

Ali: Hi, Lee! What's wrong? You look depressed.

Lee: Ah, Ali. You know that girl in my Dance Club, Reema?

Ali: Sure I do! You never stop talking about her!

Lee: I want to ask her out, but I'm too nervous!

Ali: Oh, c'mon, Lee. You and she have a good time dancing together, don't you?

Lee: I think so. We have a lot of fun together.

Ali: That means she likes you, buddy!

Question 3. *What does Ali think?*

Lee: So, I should ask her out?

Ali: Of course!

Lee: All right! I'll do it!

Conversation 4

Reema: Lee, I always have so much fun dancing with you! You really are a good dancer!

Lee: Thanks, Reema. I… I… like dancing with you, too. But…

Reema: But what? What's wrong?

Lee: Nothing, but I want to ask you something and I don't know how.

Reema: Well, why don't we have some coffee after the dance? You can ask me then!

Question 4. *What just happened?*

Lee: You mean you want to go out … with me?

Reema: Of course! I just had to finally ask you!

Conversation 5

Peter: Great party, isn't it?

Dina: Yes, it is.

Peter: I'm Peter, by the way.

Dina: Hi, Peter. I'm Dina.

Peter: Nice to meet you! Are you a student at Faber College, too?

Dina: Yes, I am. I'm a business major

Peter: Really? Me, too! Say, would you like to get some coffee after the party?

Dina: Oh, thanks, Peter, but I'm leaving soon and going home.

Peter: Well, how about having lunch sometime next week?

Dina: Gosh, Peter, I don't know how to say this, but…

Question 5.
What is Dina probably going to do?

Dina: … but I really can't go out with you. My boyfriend would get upset.

| Peter: | That's OK. Nice to meet you anyway! |
| Dina: | You, too. |

 5 Listening for Main Ideas page 105

6 Listening for Specific Information
page 105

Alicia	I'm glad we could get together for lunch, Lee!
Lee:	Me, too. So, what's this party you texted me about?
Alicia:	Sssh! It's a secret!… a surprise party!
Lee:	Really? Whose birthday is it?
Alicia:	Beth's!
Lee:	And when is it?
Alicia:	Next Friday night at my place. Can you come?
Lee:	I'd love to! Do you want me to bring anything, I mean, besides a present for Beth?
Alicia:	Yes, please. It's going to be a potluck, so can you bring a salad?
Lee:	OK. For how many people?
Alicia:	Enough for 15.
Lee:	Sure! And what time do you want me to be there?
Alicia:	Early! Before Beth, of course. Can you be there by 4:30? I told Beth to come at 5. I told her I was going to take her out to dinner for her birthday.
Lee:	Sounds great! So, how old is Beth going to be?
Alicia:	Lee! You know I don't give out that kind of information!

8 Preparing to Listen to Invitations
page 106

Example 1

| Beth: | Can you come to my sister's wedding next month? |

Example 2

| Dan: | Thanks so much for inviting me! I really wish I could, but I'll be away. |

Questions:

1. I'm having a get-together at my place tomorrow night. Can you come?
2. Sure! I'd love to come!
3. I'd really like to, but I'm busy.
4. Would you like to come over this Friday for dinner?
5. How about some pizza after class today?
6. I wish I could, but I'm doing something then.

9 Listening for Main Ideas page 107

10 Listening for Specific Information
page 107

Conversation 1

Yuri:	I'm having a graduation party after the ceremony next Sunday. I'd love for you to come!
Sandrine:	Oh, I'd love to, but my brother is having a graduation party that day too.
Yuri:	That's too bad. Will you be at the ceremony?
Sandrine:	Yes, I'll see you at the ceremony. I'm sorry I'll miss your party!

Conversation 2

Rosa:	So, Doug, you know my older sister, Liz, right?
Doug:	Of course! I met her last month at your party.
Rosa:	Well, she's getting married!
Doug:	Really? That's great! When?
Rosa:	Next June. And my sister is inviting you to the wedding! Can you come?
Doug:	Oh, gosh, Rosa. I really wish I could, but remember, I'm going to be away in Spain this summer, so I can't.

Conversation 3

| Joey: | Hi, Lisa! My Entrepreneurs' Club is having a picnic at the beach next Saturday afternoon. Would you like to come? |
| Lisa: | I'd like to, Joey, but I have to study next Saturday until at least 3:30. |

Ali: That's OK. Call me when you finish studying. The picnic will be all day and evening and you'll be hungry.

Lisa: You're right! OK, then I'll go!

Conversation 4

Patrice: Amanda, how about some pizza after class today?

Amanda: Sorry, Patrice, we're going on a hike with the Hiking Club, remember?

Patrice: I remember! But let's have pizza after the hike!

Amanda: Sure! I'd like that!

CHAPTER **6** **Sleep and Dreams**

PART 1 Conversation: Sleep Deprived

8 **Listening for Stressed Words** page 116

Beth: Ali! What's the matter? You look so sleepy!

Alicia: Yeah! Can't you wake up this morning?

Ali: No, I can't! I can hardly keep my eyes open! I was up late last night. My friend had a party. I only got about four hours of sleep.

Alicia: Why didn't you sleep in this morning?

Ali: I have to meet my study group at the library. We have a big test next week.

Beth: A big test? Why didn't you study last night instead of going to the party?

Ali: Oh, it's OK. I studied a lot before the party.

Alicia: Maybe that's not a good idea.

Ali: Why not?

Alicia: I read a research study. It said that if you don't get enough sleep after you study, you may forget 30 percent of what you studied! Especially if you studied something that is very complex.

Ali: Thirty percent? That's almost one third!

Beth: Yes, that's a lot. Are you sure, Alicia?

Alicia: Yes. Even two days after you study— if you don't get enough sleep, you forget a lot. It's called being "sleep-deprived."

Beth: Well, I read that eating right can help you study.

Ali: You mean what you eat helps you study?

Beth: Yes, there are chemicals that help you stay alert. I think the best foods are fish, eggs, soy, rice, and peanuts. So you should get enough sleep and eat the right foods.

Ali: That sounds like good advice! I'll see you two later!

Alicia: Where are you going, Ali?

Ali: Home to take a nap!

10 **Distinguishing Between Teens and Tens** page 117

1. He is <u>forty</u> years old.

2. I bought <u>thirteen</u> new books.

3. The price is <u>seventeen</u> dollars.

4. It happened in <u>1918</u>.

5. We stayed for <u>fifty</u> days.

6. I live at <u>60</u> New Hope Road.

PART 2 Using Language

Lee: Alicia, how many hours a night do you sleep?

Alicia: Usually nine or ten.

Lee: Wow! That's a lot!

Alicia: I don't think so. I think people need different amounts of sleep.

Lee: Maybe you're right, but I read that eight hours is normal for most people.

Alicia: Perhaps that's the average, but don't you think that everyone is different?

Lee: I'm not sure. Eight hours seems like plenty to me.

Alicia: How many hours do you sleep?

Lee: Usually five or six.

Alicia: Five or six! No wonder you think nine is too much!

PART 3   Listening

1 Using Context Clues page 123

Part 1

Good morning, class. I hope you all had enough sleep last night. If you read the chapter, you know that the topic for today is "Sleep and the Human Brain." First, I will review the importance of sleep. Then I will tell you about some new research on sleep and studying. Finally, I will discuss the health benefits of sleep.

Question 1: *What are you listening to?*

This lecture will cover some of the information in your textbook and add some new information.

Part 2

We don't know why the human brain needs sleep. We do know that sleep is important for physical health and mental health. Your body needs sleep to stay healthy and strong. Your brain seems to need sleep for the same reason.

Question 2: *What does sleep do for your brain?*

Sleep helps your brain stay healthy. It helps you think clearly and remember more.

Part 3

Carlyle Smith, a psychology professor in Canada, did some research on sleep. He studied how sleep affects memory. He started by teaching students two things: first, a list of words, and second, a difficult problem.

Question 3: *Why did Carlyle Smith teach the students a list of words and a difficult problem?*

Then Smith tested the students to see how much they remembered of the list of words and the problem.

Part 4

Before he gave the students the test, he asked the students to sleep different amounts for the next three nights. Some students slept eight hours every night. Some students only slept four hours the first night; then they slept eight hours the next two nights. Some students slept eight hours the first night, only four hours the second night, and eight hours the third night. Some students slept eight hours the first night and eight hours the second night, but only four hours the third night.

Question 4: *Why did Smith have the students sleep different amounts on the first, second, and third nights?*

Smith wanted to see if sleeping only a few hours for three nights after learning something new affects the memory.

Part 5

The results of the research showed that people remember better when they get enough sleep. Of course, the students who slept eight hours every night did the best on the test. They remembered the list of words and the difficult problem very well. The students who slept only four hours the second night after learning the words and the problem also did very well. But the results were very different for the students who slept only four hours on the first night or the third night.

Question 5: *How did the students who didn't sleep much on the first or third nights remember the difficult problem?*

Students who didn't sleep much on the first and third nights did not do well on the test or the difficult problem. They couldn't remember how to solve the problem. Smith concluded that it is very important to sleep enough the night after you learn something new and the third night after—but it might be safe to stay up late on the second night!

5 **Listening for Main Ideas** page 125

6 **Listening for Details** page 125

Carlyle Smith's study on memory and sleep showed some interesting results. There were four subject groups of students in the study. All the students learned a list of words and how to solve a complex problem. The first group of students slept eight hours a night for three nights after learning the new material. One week later, they took a test on the words and the problem. They remembered all the material. Most scored 100 percent on both tests—on the list of words and the complex problem.

The second subject group only slept four hours the night after learning the material—they were sleep-deprived the first night. One week later, they still remembered the list of words, but they didn't remember how to solve the complex problem. Most scored 100 percent on the list of words, but only 70 percent on the complex problem.

The third subject group was sleep-deprived the second night after learning the new material. Strangely, they scored just as well as the first group. Most answered 98 percent of the questions correctly on both tests—the list of words and the complex problem.

The fourth group slept well the first and second night, but they were sleep-deprived on the third night. This group had the same memory problems as the group that was sleep-deprived on the first night. They remembered the list of words, but not how to solve the problem. Their scores on the tests were the same as the second group.

11 **Listening for Main Ideas** page 127

12 **Listening to a Dream** page 128

Ali: I had the strangest dream last night! I was going to the movies with Beth. I went to her apartment to get her. When I arrived, Beth was wearing normal clothes. I was also wearing normal clothes, too, but I was also wearing flippers and a face mask without a bathing suit. Beth said, "Ali, take off that face mask! I can't see your face." I tried to take the mask off, but I couldn't take it off. Then I tried to take the flippers off, but my arms couldn't move. Beth tried to help me take the mask off, but she couldn't take it off either. Then, she tried to help me take off my flippers. She pulled on a flipper and I fell backwards and I broke a vase. I was so embarrassed!

CHAPTER **7** **Work and Lifestyles**

PART 1 Conversation: Looking for a Summer Job

4 **Listening for Main Ideas** page 136

5 **Listening for Specific Information (Part 1)** page 136

6 **Listening for Specific Information (Part 2)** page 136

8 **Listening for Stressed Words** page 138

Alicia: Thanks for coming with me to the Placement Center, Ali.

Ali: Don't mention it! It's nice to have your company. Besides, I need to find a summer job, too!

Alicia: What kind of job are you looking for, Ali?

Ali: I'm hoping to find one in my major, public health.

Alicia: I'm sure you can. Do you have any experience in public health?

Ali: Yes, I do. I worked part-time in a lab in Maryland last summer.

Alicia: That's great. I want to find a job writing for a local newspaper. I'd like to be a reporter.

Ali: Your major's journalism, isn't it?

Alicia: Uh-huh. I had a great job last summer when I was in Mexico City.

Ali:	Really? What did you do?
Alicia:	I worked part-time for *Excelsior*. It's the biggest newspaper in Mexico.
Ali:	What did you do there?
Alicia:	I wrote local news stories—you know—news about Mexico City. But someday I want to write international news stories. Then I can travel around the world and find out what people are like in other places.
Ali:	That sounds wonderful. I'm sure you can do it.
Alicia:	Are there any jobs in public health on the bulletin board?
Ali:	No, I don't see anything interesting.
Alicia:	You should try looking on the Web. There are some great job sites. That's how I found the job in Mexico City.
Ali:	That's a good idea. Do I search for "public health"?
Alicia:	Try "jobs in public health" or the names of specific jobs. I searched for "newspaper reporter."
Ali:	I'll go to the computer lab right now and try that! See you later.

10 Distinguishing between Majors and Job Titles page 130

1. He's a journalist.
2. I study economics.
3. Elizabeth is a psychologist.
4. Are you an accountant?
5. I majored in biology.
6. She's a physicist.
7. Do you study chemistry?

PART 2   Using Language

2 Listening for Main Ideas page 142

3 Listening for Specific Information page 142

Ann:	Uh-h-h, Paula, may I speak to you for a minute?
Paula:	Sure, Ann. What is it?
Ann:	I'm having a problem with one of the other account managers. She's always late for work, so I have to do her work, too.
Paula:	Did you discuss this with her?
Ann:	I talked to her last week, but she is still coming late every day. I had to make a presentation to a client for her this morning.
Paula:	Well, let's talk to her together and see if we can come up with a solution. Meet me in my office at three o'clock.
Ann:	Thanks, Paula.

PART 3   Listening

2 Using Context Clues page 144

Conversation 1

Interviewer:	Come in!
Alicia:	Excuse me. May I see you now? I have an appointment.
Interviewer:	Of course. You're . . . Alicia?
Alicia:	Yes, that's right. Alicia Morales.
Interviewer:	And you're interested in working for us?
Alicia:	Yes. I have some experience. I was a part-time reporter last summer for *Excelsior*.
Interviewer:	I see. Well, this sample of your writing is excellent.

Question 1: *Who is Alicia talking to?*

Interviewer:	As manager of our newspaper, I think we might have an opening in the international news department.
Alicia:	Oh, I hope so! I would love to work on international stories!

Conversation 2

Dan:	What are you going to do this summer, Sang-mi? Going back to Korea?

Sang-mi: I'd like to, Dan, but I have to think about my future.

Dan: Your future? What do you mean?

Sang-mi: Well, someday I want to help sick people. So I want to get some hospital experience.

Dan: You mean working part-time in one?

Sang-mi: Uh-huh.

Question 2:
What does Sang-mi want to do this summer?

Dan: If you want to work in a hospital, you should visit County General Hospital. They may have part-time summer jobs.

Sang-mi: I will. Thanks.

Conversation 3

Sang-mi: So how about you, Dan? What are your summer plans?

Dan: I'm still not sure what I'm going to do. I should study, but my friend Bill—y'know, the one in San Francisco?

Sang-mi: Oh, right.

Dan: He wants me to go with him to Europe in July and August.

Sang-mi: Really?

Dan: Yeah. I'm thinking about it.

Question 3: *What is Dan thinking about doing this summer?*

Sang-mi: That's a great plan. You *should* go to Europe this summer.

Conversation 4

Dan: Yes, but I have to think about September.

Sang-mi: Aren't you going to go back to school?

Dan: Well, I should go back. But I'm getting tired of school. I want more experience in the real world.

Sang-mi: So you want more job experience?

Dan: Uh-huh.

Question 4:
What does Dan want to do in the fall?

Sang-mi: I know how you feel. I want to work too, but I have to get out of school first.

Conversation 5

Dan: Is that because you're an international student?

Sang-mi: That's right. I can only study with my student visa, except in the summer. Then I can work part-time.

Question 5: *Can Sang-mi work?*

Dan: So you can work only in the summer? That's rough.

Sang-mi: Oh, it's not bad. But I have to be careful with money!

⑤ Listening for Main Ideas page 145

⑥ Listening for Specific Information page 145

Claudia: Rafael, your résumé is very impressive. Please tell me why you're interested in this job.

Rafael: Well, I like working with computers, and the job sounds very challenging.

Claudia: I see. Why should I give you a job with this company?

Rafael: My work is accurate, and I learn quickly. In fact, I really like learning new information and new skills!

Claudia: Good. You'll have a lot to learn here. Tell me, Rafael, what do you think you'll be doing in ten years?

Rafael: I like working with people, so I'd like to be a department manager in ten years.

⑩ Listening for Main Ideas page 147

⑪ Listening to Future Plans page 148

Father: So what are your plans for this summer, Dan?

Dan:	Well, I could work for that construction company again. But I have a great opportunity to do some traveling and learn more about the world.
Father:	What's that?
Dan:	My friend Bill is going to travel around Europe this summer—he has some relatives in France he wants to visit, and he plans to go to Germany, Lithuania, and Latvia. He'll have a rental car, so all I need to pay for is my airfare and meals.
Father:	What about hotels when you're not staying with Bill's relatives?
Dan:	We'll stay in youth hostels. They're really cheap. I have enough money saved from my part-time job.
Father:	What about money for next year? For your books and other expenses?
Dan:	Well, I'll need to borrow a little from you. But this is a once in a lifetime chance. I really think I could learn a lot, and I can improve my French, too!

CHAPTER **8** **Food and Nutrition**

PART 1 Conversation: At a Food Court

(4) **Listening for Main Ideas** page 155

(5) **Listening for Specific Information (Part 1)** page 156

(6) **Listening for Specific Information (Part 2)** page 156

(8) **Listening for Stressed Words** page 157

Dan:	Wow! Look at all these different places to eat!
Pat:	You said it! There are so many choices: American fast food, Chinese, Italian, vegetarian! I can't decide what to eat!
Meryl:	What are you going to have, Dan?
Dan:	I'm hungry! I'm going to the fast-food place. I want a double cheeseburger and a large order of fries.
Pat:	Ugh! How many cheeseburgers do you eat every week? You had a couple at the picnic yesterday, didn't you?
Dan:	Yeah... so what? I *like* cheeseburgers!
Meryl:	I think Pat's worried about you.
Dan:	Why? I'm healthy!
Pat:	But cheeseburgers have a lot of fat.
Meryl:	And a lot of calories.
Dan:	OK, OK! What are *you* going to have?
Pat:	I'm going to have some tofu and rice at that Chinese place.
Dan:	Oh, I forgot. You're a vegetarian, right?
Pat:	Right.
Meryl:	Hmm. I think I'm going to have a salad.
Dan:	Are you on a diet?
Meryl:	No diet—I just like to eat healthy food.
Dan:	What are you going to have to drink?
Meryl:	A large cola.
Dan:	A large cola? But there's lots of sugar in soda!
Pat:	Dan's right. And sugar's bad for your teeth.
Meryl:	All right! I'll have a *diet* cola. There's no sugar in that!
Dan:	Great! And *I'll* have a salad, too.

(10) **Listening for Reductions** page 158

1. What're ya gonna have?
2. I think I'm gonna have some tofu 'n rice.
3. We would like a couple of salads.
4. Isn't there a lotta fat in cheeseburgers?
5. They don't want to eat lots of fatty food.

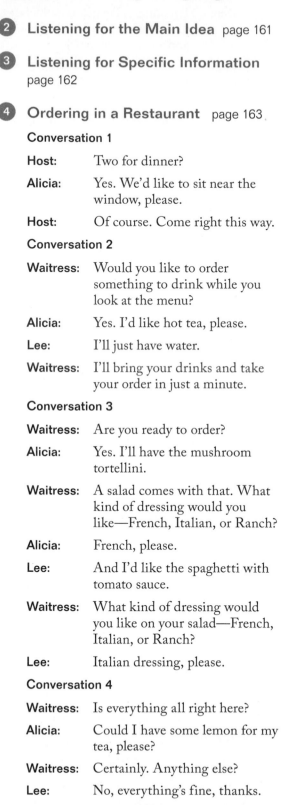

PART 2   Using Language

2 Listening for the Main Idea page 161

3 Listening for Specific Information page 162

4 Ordering in a Restaurant page 163

Conversation 1

Host: Two for dinner?

Alicia: Yes. We'd like to sit near the window, please.

Host: Of course. Come right this way.

Conversation 2

Waitress: Would you like to order something to drink while you look at the menu?

Alicia: Yes. I'd like hot tea, please.

Lee: I'll just have water.

Waitress: I'll bring your drinks and take your order in just a minute.

Conversation 3

Waitress: Are you ready to order?

Alicia: Yes. I'll have the mushroom tortellini.

Waitress: A salad comes with that. What kind of dressing would you like—French, Italian, or Ranch?

Alicia: French, please.

Lee: And I'd like the spaghetti with tomato sauce.

Waitress: What kind of dressing would you like on your salad—French, Italian, or Ranch?

Lee: Italian dressing, please.

Conversation 4

Waitress: Is everything all right here?

Alicia: Could I have some lemon for my tea, please?

Waitress: Certainly. Anything else?

Lee: No, everything's fine, thanks.

Conversation 5

Waitress: Can I get you anything else tonight? Some dessert or coffee?

Alicia: No, thank you. Just the check, please.

Waitress: Here you are. I hope you enjoyed your dinner. Come back soon.

PART 3   Listening

2 Using Context Clues page 164

Conversation 1

Lee: Everything looks delicious! What are you going to have?

Alicia: Dan says the onion soup here tastes great. I think that's what I'll have.

Lee: That sounds good.

Question 1: *Where are Lee and Alicia?*

Lee: Y'know, it's really nice to eat in a restaurant.

Alicia: It sure is.

Conversation 2

Waiter: Here you go. Was everything OK?

Alicia: Yes, thank you. Everything was delicious.

Lee: Yes, it was. But, excuse me.

Waiter: Yes?

Lee: What's this charge for?

Waiter: Hmm. Let me see. Oh, yes. That's for your drinks. One hot tea, $1.85, and one cola, $2.25.

Question 2: *What's Lee asking about?*

Lee: Oh, I see. Thanks for explaining the bill.

Waiter: You're welcome, sir.

Conversation 3

Beth: Now, Dan. What's next?

Dan: Hmm. Just a minute. Ah,… one cup of milk.

Beth: A cup of milk.

Dan: One teaspoon of salt.

Beth: A teaspoon of salt.

Dan: And one egg.

Beth: Right.

Dan: Beat the milk, salt, and egg mixture thoroughly and…

Question 3: *What are Dan and Beth doing?*

Dan: This is fun, isn't it?

Beth: Yes, it is. I really enjoy cooking.

Dan: But eating is even better!

Conversation 4

Ali: Wow! This place is really big!

Alicia: It *is* big, isn't it?

Ali: Look at all this food.

Alicia: Here's what we need for the salad. What's on the list?

Ali: Let's see—lettuce, tomatoes, carrots, and cucumbers.

Question 4: *Where are Ali and Alicia?*

Ali: All these fruits and vegetables look so fresh!

Alicia: Yeah. These big supermarkets have good produce!

Conversation 5

Ali: So, do we have everything on the shopping list?

Alicia: I think so. Oh! We need spaghetti sauce. It's over there…

Ali: Here it is. What kind should we buy?

Alicia: Hmm. Here's one… spaghetti sauce with mushrooms… eight ounces, $1.06.

Ali: That looks good. But here's another kind. It's only 99 cents.

Alicia: Really? Let me see the label… spaghetti sauce with mushrooms… oh, but look *here*, Ali. There's only six ounces in this one.

Question 5:
Which spaghetti sauce is the best price?

Ali: Oh yeah, you're right. The eight-ounce size for $1.06 is the best price. Let's buy that one.

⑤ Listening for Main Ideas page 165

⑥ Listening to Instructions page 165

Ali: Beth, Alicia—I'm so happy to see you! I need some help.

Beth: What's the problem, Ali?

Ali: Well, you know I never cooked before I came to the university.

Alicia: Uh-huh.

Ali: I asked my mother for some recipes so I can make my favorite dishes. She sent me these, but I don't understand the instructions.

Beth: We can try to help, Ali. What are the instructions you don't understand?

Ali: First it says to "chop" some onions. How do I do that?

Alicia: "Chop" just means to cut them up into very small pieces with a knife.

Ali: Oh, OK. I get it. Now this one says to "brown" the onions.

Beth: That means to cook them in a little oil until they turn brown all over.

Ali: I've never seen "brown" as a verb before! This one, "mix thoroughly," I understand. It means to mix the things together completely, right?

Beth: Right.

Ali: What about this—"grate" the cheese? How do I grate cheese?

Alicia: You need a special tool for that—a cheese grater. It has little holes and sharp points on it so that when you rub the cheese over it, thin bits of the cheese fall through the holes. Then you can put the cheese on top of other foods like pizza. I have a cheese grater you can borrow.

Ali: Great! Thanks a lot. I'll invite you for dinner when I finish!

⑩ Listening for the Main Idea page 168

⑪ Ordering Steps in a Recipe page 168

Wally Chan: Hi. I'm Wally Chan. Welcome

to *Chan Cooks*. Today I'm making chili. You make chili with beans, beef, and tomatoes.

First, you chop an onion. Cut it into small pieces. Then, brown the onion and some ground beef in a little oil. Cook the onion and beef in the oil until the onion is a little brown, and the beef is all brown. Now, add tomatoes and chili powder to the beef and onion. Chili powder is hot, so just use a little if you don't like spicy food. Cook this mixture for about an hour, stirring occasionally.

OK. Here's what it looks like when it's done. I like to serve the chili in a bowl with some shredded cheese on top. Enjoy!

12 Discussing Opinions About Food page 169

1. I like onions on my hamburgers.

2. Chili powder makes food too hot and spicy.

3. I eat a lot of cheese—with crackers, bread, and other foods.

4. Tomatoes are best in salad, with lettuce, oil, and vinegar.

5. I like beans when they are cooked with onions and garlic.

6. Cooking with oil can make you fat.

7. The best pizza has just tomato sauce and lots of cheese.

8. Foods like beans, rice, and potatoes should be eaten at every meal.

9. Onions are good cooked and uncooked.

10. I like a lot of salt in my food.

CHAPTER 9 Great Destinations

PART 1 Conversation: Arriving in San Francisco

4 Listening for Main Ideas (Part 1) page 178

5 Listening for Main Ideas (Part 2) page 178

6 Listening for Specific Information page 179

8 Listening for Stressed Words page 181

Beth: Look, guys, up ahead! There's San Francisco! We're almost there!

Ali: Look at that skyline! What's that tall, triangular building? It looks like a tower.

Dan: That's the Transamerica Building. It's one of San Francisco's landmarks. It's almost as famous now as the Golden Gate Bridge, the cable cars, Chinatown…

Ali: Well, I can't wait to go to all those places… and Alcatraz, too.

Beth: You said it! Alcatraz used to be the prison where the most dangerous criminals in the United States were put. Now, it's a really interesting former prison and great place to tour.

Dan: Let's try to go there tomorrow. Then, we can also do something else tomorrow. Uh-oh!

Beth: Dan! What's wrong with the car?

Ali: Yeah! Why are we going slower?

Dan: *Oh, no!* I think we have a flat tire!

Beth: We have a spare tire, don't we?

Dan: Yes, I think so. I'll pull over… There it is. It *is* a flat tire. Now, who can help me change it?

Beth and Ali: I can!

Beth: I can't believe we have a flat tire … and just before we got to San Francisco!

Ali: Oh, it'll take us just a few minutes to change it. Then, we can start to explore the city!

PART 2 Using Language

 2 **Listening for Main Ideas** page 184

3 **Listening for Specific Information**
page 185

Conversation 1

Lee: Ali, it's a perfect day to go to the beach. Let's go!

Ali: I think it's a little too cold to spend a day at the beach. I'd rather go on a bike ride. Come and ride to the Prospect Park Lake with me. We can stop for ice cream on the way back.

Lee: OK. That sounds good. I'll get my bike.

Conversation 2

Alicia: Hey, Beth. Do you want to go shopping at the mall today?

Beth: I think I've been spending too much money lately. Wouldn't you rather go for a nice walk in the mountains? It's free!

Alicia: You're right. We should get more exercise. Let me put on my walking shoes and we can go.

Conversation 3

Dan: Ming, should we go out to dinner tonight?

Ming: Sure, Dan. Where do you want to go?

Dan: Well, I have some menus here. There's a new Mexican restaurant on Poplar. Let's go there.

Ming: Oh, I ate there last night. It was a little too spicy for me. Couldn't we go to Wang's instead?

Dan: I guess so. Chinese is good, too. Let's go!

PART 3 Listening

2 **Using Context Clues** page 189

Conversation 1

Beth: Well, we've got everything in the trunk.

Dan: I thought the tent wasn't going to fit!

Ali: The sleeping bags and fishing equipment take up a lot of space, too.

Beth: You guys have too much luggage, too.

Question 1. *What did Beth, Dan, and Ali finish doing?*

Beth: We just got everything in the car, and it's already almost lunchtime!

Conversation 2

Dan: Yes, so let's go find something to eat.

Beth: Where? There's not a town or restaurant anywhere near here.

Ali: Yes, there is. Look at this map. There's a town about five miles from here.

Dan: You're right! Let's go!

Question 2. *What are Beth, Dan, and Ali going to do?*

Beth: I'm so glad there's a town near here. It must have a restaurant or two. I'm really hungry!

Conversation 3

Ali: Well, that was a great lunch.

Beth: Yeah, we were lucky to find such a good restaurant way out here.

Dan: Thanks to you and your map!

Ali: Nah, it was easy. Say, why is it so dark outside?

Beth: Look at that sky! I don't like this. It's really cloudy.

Dan: You're right. I'll turn on the radio.

Question 3. *Why is Dan going to turn on the radio?*

Ali: Yes, see if you can find a weather report.

Conversation 4

Radio: … and in southern New Mexico, there's a flash flood advisory through this evening with a 50 percent chance of rain this afternoon, increasing to 70 percent tonight. Lows expected tonight near freezing.

Question 4. *What's the weather probably going to be like tonight?*

Beth: Did you hear *that*? It's going to be really rainy and cold tonight.

Conversation 5

Ali: Maybe this is the night for us to stay in a motel.

Dan: I think so, too. Camping's fun but not in the rain. Ah! We're almost in the town. Let's see if there's a motel.

Beth: Dan! Why didn't you stop?

Ali: Yeah! Didn't you see the sign? You could get a ticket!

Dan: No, I didn't! Sorry, guys!

Question 5. *Why is Dan sorry?*

Beth: Phew! Be *careful*, Dan!

Dan: You're right. I didn't even see that stop sign.

5 Listening for Main Ideas page 190

Tour Guide: This is the capitol building for the state of Georgia. The capitol building is famous for its gold roof. The gold came from the mountains of Georgia.

Just east of the capitol building, in downtown Atlanta, is the Martin Luther King, Jr., National Historic Site. It's a memorial to Martin Luther King, Jr., the great leader of the American Civil Rights Movement. Martin Luther King, Jr., was from Atlanta. His grave is at this site.

Now, we're just east of the city of Atlanta. This is Stone Mountain. It's a natural hill of stone. It's famous because a man carved an image of three Civil War generals on the side of the mountain. These generals are Jefferson Davis, Robert E. Lee, and Stonewall Jackson.

Now we're coming around to Interstate Highway I-20, to the west side of the city. This is Six Flags Amusement Park. It's a large amusement park with lots of roller coasters and other rides.

6 Listening for Places on a Map
page 191

7 Listening for Details page 191

Number 1

Tour Guide: This is the capitol building for the state of Georgia. The capitol building is famous for its gold roof. The gold came from the mountains of Georgia.

Number 2

Tour Guide: Just east of the capitol building, in downtown Atlanta, is the Martin Luther King, Jr., National Historic Site. It's a memorial to Martin Luther King, Jr., the great leader of the American Civil Rights Movement. Martin Luther King, Jr., was from Atlanta. His grave is at this site.

Number 3

Tour Guide: Now, we're just east of the city of Atlanta. This is Stone Mountain. It's a natural hill of stone. It's famous because a man carved an image of three Civil War generals on the side of the mountain. These generals are Jefferson Davis, Robert E. Lee, and Stonewall Jackson.

Number 4

Tour Guide: Now we're coming around to Interstate Highway I-20, to the west side of the city. This is Six Flags Amusement Park. It's a large amusement park with lots of roller coasters and other rides.

10 Listening for the Main Idea page 192

11 Listening for Specific Information
page 193

Travel Agent: Yes, what can I do for you?

Alicia: I'd like to go to Walt Disney World, so I need information on flights to Florida.

Agent: OK. I think I can get a good fare for you to Orlando, Florida. Do you want to go first class, business class, or economy?

Alicia: Oh, economy, of course. I'd like the lowest fare you can find.

Agent: All right. And that's one way or round trip?

Alicia:	Round trip. I'd like to leave on Sunday the 12th and return on Saturday the 18th.
Agent:	Well, there's a very low fare on Sunday morning. It's only $145, but it's not direct. You have to change planes in Atlanta. There's a direct, nonstop flight, but the fare on that one is $680.
Alicia:	That's OK. I'll change planes in Atlanta
Agent:	OK. That's Flight 690. It departs at 8:15 A.M. on Sunday the 12th and arrives in Orlando at 12:15.
Alicia:	That sounds good.
Agent:	Oh, there's one more thing. It's a special low fare, so the ticket is nonrefundable.
Alicia:	That's all right. I'm not going to change my plans.

CHAPTER **10**	**Our Planet**

PART 1 Conversation: Earth Day

① Listening for Main Ideas page 202

⑤ Listening for Specific Information (Part 1) page 202

⑥ Listening for Specific Information (Part 2) page 203

⑧ Listening for Stressed Words page 204

Alicia:	Come in!
Lee:	Hi, Alicia. How's it going?
Alicia:	Hi, Lee. I'm fine… but busy!
Lee:	What are you doing?
Alicia:	I'm making a sign for Earth Day.
Lee:	*Earth Day*? What's that?

Alicia:	On Earth Day, people think about pollution and other problems with the environment.
Lee:	Really! When is Earth Day?
Alicia:	Next Monday.
Lee:	… and is it every year?
Alicia:	Yes, it is. The first Earth Day was in 1970, and now it happens every year, on April 22nd. On that day, people talk and learn about problems with the environment.
Lee:	… like, how?
Alicia:	Well, one year, thousands of people came to Washington, D.C., to support clean energy. In Italy, 150 towns and cities had Car-less Weekends when nobody could drive.
Lee:	You mean Earth Day happens all over the world?
Alicia:	Yes, it sure does! Earth Day happens in many countries.
Lee:	And what's going on here at the college?
Alicia:	There's a lot happening at the college. At the student union, there will be exhibits on pollution… Students will also plant some trees around the college campus.
Lee:	So, what are you planning to do on Earth Day?
Alicia:	I'm planning to give a speech about pollution. Also, I'm going to carry this sign.
Lee:	What does it say? *Save the Earth!* That's great, Alicia. Can I go with you and help? I want to help the environment too.
Alicia:	Sure, Lee. Would *you* like to carry a sign too?
Lee:	Yes, I sure would!

⑨ Listening for Emphasis page 205

Conversation 1

Alicia:	Some people think air pollution is a big problem, but others think progress is more important.

Lee: Well, what do *you* think about pollution?

Conversation 2

Alicia: Air pollution and water pollution are two serious environmental problems.

Lee: Do you think *air pollution* is the biggest problem?

Conversation 3

Alicia: One of the things I do on Earth Day is to stop driving my car.

Lee: Will you ride your *bicycle* to school on Earth Day?

Conversation 4

Alicia: We're going to plant trees all over town on Earth Day. We have 500 trees to plant.

Lee: How many trees will you plant on *campus*?

Conversation 5

Alicia: Students from the college are going to clean up Audubon Park, Haley Park, Finley Park, and Tom Lee Park.

Lee: Which parks are *you* going to clean up?

PART 2   Using Language

1 Listening for Main Ideas page 208

2 Listening for Opinions page 208

Amy: Air pollution is so bad in this city! I think the local government should stop people from driving cars on certain days.

Nabil: You have a point. Air pollution is a problem, but not letting people drive on certain days is a bad idea. People need their cars to get to work, and trucks need to deliver goods to stores.

Amy: I'm afraid I don't agree with you there. Saving the environment is too important. People are so used to driving that they don't think of other ways to do things. If we stopped people from driving on certain days,

maybe we could think of new ways to get around.

Nabil: I understand your point of view, but I still think it wouldn't be possible to stop people from driving.

PART 3   Listening

1 Using Context Clues page 210

Speaker 1

Speaker 1: In my opinion, it's very dangerous to walk on the streets at night. Someone might steal your money—or even hurt you. The police should do more to stop this problem.

Question 1.
What problem is Speaker 1 talking about?

Speaker 1: Because of crime, I'm afraid. I want to leave this city.

Speaker 2

Speaker 2: I agree that crime is a problem, but the problem with the air is even bigger. Every day I look out the window, and the sky is brown and dirty. People shouldn't drive so much. And the factories should run in a cleaner way.

Question 2: *What does Speaker 2 think is a bigger problem than crime?*

Speaker 2: Air pollution here is really bad. The city *must* do something to clean up the air.

Speaker 3

Speaker 3: I agree that crime and air pollution are serious problems. But we shouldn't forget what we have to drink. The rivers are dirty, the city water isn't safe, and I have to buy my water in bottles. Even the rain isn't good for the trees and plants.

Question 3: *What does Speaker 3 think is another serious problem?*

Speaker 3: I think crime and air pollution *are* big problems, but water pollution is a big problem, too.

Speaker 4

Speaker 4: I agree with Speakers 1, 2, and 3 that crime and pollution are serious in the city. But to me, just driving from one place to another is the most serious problem. I drive five miles to work, but it takes me half an hour because the traffic is so bad. Every year, there are more cars, trucks, and buses. Then when I go shopping, I have to wait in line for ten or twenty minutes just to pay! There are few too services for too many people.

Question 4: *What does Speaker 4 think is the most serious problem in the city?*

Speaker 4: In my opinion, overcrowding is worse than crime and pollution.

Speaker 5

Speaker 5: It's good to talk about local problems, but I think it's important not to forget the big picture. The cities are only one part of a much bigger problem. We have to find answers to the biggest problem of all— protecting and preserving the Earth.

Question 5: *What does Speaker 5 think is the biggest problem of all?*

Speaker 5: In other words, we have to understand that problems aren't only in the cities but also in the whole environment.

4 **Listening for the Main Idea (Part 1)** page 211

5 **Listening for Main Ideas (Part 2)** page 211

6 **Listening for Details** page 211

Message 1

It takes about 17 mature trees to clean the air of the pollution from one automobile. Give the trees a break on Earth Day and ride your bike or take a free shuttle bus to the Earth Fair in Marquette Park on Monday, April 22nd. Call 555-1234 for information.

Message 2

What can you do to save the planet on Earth Day? Bring your recyclables to the Earth Fair recycling center at Marquette Park on Monday, April 22nd, from 10 A.M. to 5 P.M.

Message 3

Less than one out of every quarter million slaughtered animals is tested for toxic chemical residues. On Earth Day, eat chemical-free treats at the natural foods area at the Earth Fair in Marquette Park on Monday, April 22nd.

Message 4:

A full gallon of water can run out of your faucet in less than sixty seconds! To celebrate Earth Day, turn off the water when you brush your teeth and come to the Earth Fair in Marquette Park on Monday, April 22nd.

Message 5:

One quarter-pound hamburger represents the killing of 55 square feet of rain forest, the loss of 10 pounds of topsoil, the use of 650 gallons of water, and the introduction of 500 pounds of carbon dioxide into the atmosphere. Save the planet and eat delicious veggie burgers at the natural foods area at the Earth Fair, Monday, April 22nd, at Marquette Park.

Vocabulary Index

Chapter 1

Chapter 2

Chapter 3

Chapter 4

Chapter 5

sound like
stuff
surprise party
take someone to dinner
team
text
twice
until
wedding

Chapter 6

advice
alert
can't keep one's eyes open
chemicals
complex
deprived
hardly
percent
research study
sleep in
sleep-deprived
solve
subject group
take a nap
wake up

Chapter 7

(one's) company
accurate
appointment
challenging
client
come up with
construction
discuss
Don't mention it.
expenses
experience
find out
full-time
get out of
impressive
journalism
once in a lifetime
part-time
presentation
public health
relatives
reporter
résumé
rough
tired of
youth hostels

Chapter 8

an order of
beat
brown
calories
carrot
charge
check
cheese grater
chop cucumber
decide
dessert
diet
dressing
good/bad for you
grate
hot tea
menu
mushroom
onion soup
order
ounce
picnic
produce
rice
teaspoon
thoroughly
tofu
vegetarian
worried about
You said it!

Chapter 9

advisory
arrive
business class
can't wait
change (a tire)
change planes
coach class
Couldn't we…
criminal
depart
direct
explore
first class
fishing equipment
flash flood
flat tire
freezing
I'd rather…
landmark
Let's

luggage
nonrefundable
nonstop
one way
one-way (ticket)
prison
pull over
round trip
round-trip (ticket)
should
skyline
sleeping bag
Sounds good/OK
spare tire
take up space
tent
the way back
tower
triangular
trunk
Wouldn't you rather…

Chapter 10

a lot going on
campus
carbon dioxide
endangered species
environment
exhibit
faucet
give a speech
mature
plant
pollute
pollution
recyclables
recycle
shuttle bus
slaughtered
student union
support
topsoil
toxic chemicals
veggie (vegetable)

Skills Index